Colophon

This book was prepared on a MacBook Pro running the Adobe Design Premium Creative Suite 4. Layout was done in InDesign. Vector illustrations were created in Illustrator. Photo and image retouching was done in Photoshop. Screen shots were taken using Ambrosia's SnapzPro. Fonts used were Chapparal Pro, Myriad Pro, and European Pi 3. GridIron Flow was used to track use and versions of graphics and layout files.

Dedicated to:

My students. You ask the right questions to help me understand the answers.

FROM DESIGN INTO PRINT

Preparing Graphics and Text for Professional Printing

by Sandee Cohen

 Peachpit Press

From Design Into Print: Preparing Graphics and Text for Professional Printing

Sandee Cohen

Peachpit Press
1249 Eighth Street
Berkeley, CA 94710
510/524-2178
510/524-2221 (fax)

Find us on the Web at: www.peachpit.com
To report errors, please send a note to errata@peachpit.com
Peachpit Press is a division of Pearson Education.

Project Editor: Becky Morgan
Production Editor: Hilal Sala
Copyeditor: Dave Awl
Indexer: Valerie Haynes Perry
Cover design: Mimi Heft
Interior design: Mimi Heft
Layout: Sandee Cohen

ISBN-13: 978-0-321-49220-3

ISBN-10: 0-321-49220-X

9 8 7 6 5 4 3 2

Printed and bound in the United States of America

Introduction

This is the book I wish I had had twenty years ago, when I first started working with computer graphics. Back then, it didn't take long to realize that as soon as I put anything down on the page, I was acting as a production manager in addition to the designer or layout person. Just defining a color meant I needed to understand what the requirements were for color separations. Working with a photograph required an understanding of that strange concept called resolution. And then there were all those questions about the difference between RGB and CMYK colors.

During my years in advertising, I relied on the book, *Pocket Pal, A Graphic Arts Production Handbook*, published by the International Paper Corporation. The book was given out for free by International Paper representatives when they visited ad agencies. It covered all parts of the printing and publishing process and even had a page of proofreaders' marks. I loved leafing through the pages reading about halftone screens, impositions, separations, and other parts of printing documents.

Back in those days, however, *Pocket Pal* covered almost no digital or computer graphics. Digital cameras, scanners, and computer graphics were missing from its pages. That's when I thought there needed to be a book that covered the same topics as *Pocket Pal,* but did it from the point of view of the digital artist or designer. And would be written in a friendlier, more fun, style.

The Non-Designer's Books

In 1994, Robin Williams, author of *The Mac is not a typewriter*, came out with *The Non-Designer's Design Book*. The concept was brilliant. Since desktop publishing had made it easier for those without formal design training to create business cards, advertising, brochures, and other printed projects, Robin wrote a book that helped these non-designers learn to look at the page in design terms.

I met up with Robin at a computer event and told her that the Non-Designer's concept was great. But she should now do a Non-Designer's book on prepress and production. Robin liked the idea and some time later, she and I began work on *The Non-Designer's Scan and Print Book*.

The Non-Designer's Scan and Print Book

The idea behind the book was simple. We would create a book for all those non-designers who didn't have a clue about production and explain how to best create their digital files.

We also expanded the book slightly out of the Non-Designer's series to include real designers who also had no idea how to prepare their files for the print shop. They were puzzled why their graphics wound up looking jagged or the text was hard to read in the final printed project.

In 1999, the book was published by Peachpit Press with great reviews and feedback. Designers thanked us for writing a book that helped them talk to print shops and production managers. It answered the questions they had been too embarrassed to ask. Production managers thanked us for a book they could give to their designers. And computer graphics teachers told us how great the book was for their classes — high school, college, and adult ed.

I was thrilled. And for over seven years we didn't have to do anything in regards to the book. It practically sold itself. But around 2006, it became clear that the book needed updating. It wasn't that parts of it were wrong, it was that advances in computer graphics had made many concepts out of date.

Showing its age

Looking through the original book in 2006, it was very obvious that it was no longer topical. For instance, software had changed dramatically. All through the book we spoke about QuarkXPress and PageMaker. XPress was the dominant program in the industry while PageMaker was just hanging on. We had to mention both equally. Adobe and Macromedia had competing vector illustration programs called Illustrator and FreeHand which also needed equal treatment.

The book covered scanning in great detail, but the information on digital cameras was sparse. Few people used digital cameras back then and the concept of a camera phone was out of a Dick Tracy cartoon.

And in an effort to save production costs, the book had been printed in two colors. This had made some topics, especially the chapters on color theory, hard to explain.

It was time for an update.

Updating for the twenty-first century

Since Robin was now involved with other projects, I took on the task of rewriting the book myself. First thing Peachpit and I did was agree that it would be printed in full color. Not just a color insert, but four-color throughout the book. This made the book even better than my old *Pocket Pal*, which only had a twelve-page color insert and two colors for the rest of the pages.

We then decided to change the title. All along I had to explain to people not to let the *Non-Designer's* label throw them off. The book was most definitely for professional designers. After a lot of discussion we came up with *From Design Into Print*. It meant that once you have a design, you now needed instruction on how to get it to print well. That covered both designers and non-designers, which was always my original idea.

I also needed to change the emphasis of some of the chapters. Scanning, which used to be a very important topic, would be covered in far less detail. But working with digital cameras was expanded into its own chapter. After all, it's hard to find anyone who doesn't have a digital camera or camera phone.

In the time since the first edition, PDF has become an important part of sending files to be printed. Originally that was covered as a small section in the printing chapter, I spun them out into their own chapter.

And since 1999, the main page layout program, QuarkXPress, has been replaced by Adobe InDesign. And PageMaker, while still sold by Adobe, is no longer being developed for future versions. I deleted all the references to software that no longer was being sold, such as Macromedia FreeHand. (In fact, the entire Macromedia company no longer existed as it had been acquired by Adobe Systems, Inc.) I also had to delete references to outdated hardware such as Zip disks, Jaz disks, and telephone modems. It's incredible how much has changed!

How to read this book

Unlike most other computer graphics books, you don't have to be anywhere near your computer when you read this book. There are no step-by-step instructions to follow along with. You don't have to worry about if the book covers your most current version of the software. You can just sit back under a tree, lie back in the bathtub, or relax in a car and read. (You must not read the book while *driving* a car, though. That is very dangerous!) The chapters don't require any real knowledge of any software. They are just the stuff that helps you understand what goes on when your files go to print.

The order of the chapters is somewhat important. There are concepts in the early chapters that are necessary to understand before you read about others in the later chapters. However, if you do want to jump around the chapters, it won't hurt.

There is no specific software applications that I recommend. I do tell you which types of software are good for different types of projects. But I'm not getting into a XPress versus InDesign debate. Similarly, I'm not commenting on which platform you should use. Mac or PC doesn't matter to me.

I had a lot of fun with the images and figures in the chapters. Most of the images explain concepts in the text. But off on the side of the text you'll see little illustrations. Some are silly little cartoons or images that are there just to keep the pages from being too dull. I hope you enjoy them.

Quizzes and projects

At the end of many of the chapters there are simple little quizzes and projects that should help you understand the concepts covered that chapter. Please don't take them too seriously. I'm not grading you on the answers and neither should anyone using this book as part of teaching a class.

I'm just trying to help you look at printed documents in a new way. And hopefully you'll be able to create more polished layouts and designs. In fact, you might want to create your own quizzes and projects for you and your friends to master.

From Design Into Print: The podcast

I really enjoy explaining these print and prepress techniques to designers and production people. That's why I'm going to continue explaining these issues in the From Design Into Print podcast. This will be a "somewhat weekly" podcast where I'll deal with many of the topics in the book as well as new ones that will pop up. The podcasts are already up. Look for them on iTunes or go to FromDesignIntoPrint.com to download and subscribe. There will also be a blog where you and I can discuss issues.

Thanking those who have helped

There are quite a few people I need to acknowledge who have helped me on both *The Non-Designer's Scan and Print Book* as well as *From Design Into Print*.

First, and foremost, is **Robin Williams**. Without Robin's initial help and guidance, I would never have gotten the first version of the book published. Robin has a remarkable ability to speak directly to the beginning designer and eliminate their fears in working with computers and software. I only hope I have continued her calm and enjoyable tone of voice.

Nancy Davis and **Becky Morgan** of Peachpit Press, the two editors on the versions of the book. Nancy helped guide the course for the first version while Becky steered me through this second one. It's hard for an author to read critical comments but it's a lot easier when every comment is spot on. And it's much easier to make those corrections. I also need to thank **Pam Pfiffner**, who helped me start the transition from the first version to the second.

Nancy Ruenzel, and the rest of the Peachpit staff.

Hilal Sala, production manager for the book, who made sure the images would print and the chapters came out in the right order.

Mimi Heft, of Peachpit Press, for the cover design as well as the interior design.

My good friend and copy editor, **Dave Awl**. Dave has been with me on quite a few books. And during that time he has actually moved from being a proofreader to copy editor to an author of his own book. Not only does he spot all those missing commas and bad line breaks, but his comments about what he is reading are very funny. He makes it fun to go through and fix errors.

My intern, **Sunny**, a student at School of Visual Arts. Sunny came in and did a lot of work helping me with editing text and fixing bad paragraph breaks. She also chose photographs and artwork to use as illustrations in the book. She even created proposals for book covers. While it was too late in the process for her cover designs to be used, I think they are great.

So I am including them here so she has some published work to her credit. I'm looking forward to seeing her future designs.

My technical editor, **Jean-Claude Trembley** in Montreal. JC knows the most details about working with Adobe software, especially InDesign and Illustrator. And he has so many years experience in printing documents. I also need to thank **James Wamsur**, Adobe Certified Instructor and Adobe Certified Expert of Sells Printing. James did a special technical edit of Chapter 18 to make sure all that information was up to date.

Valerie Haynes Perry, for her lightning-quick work indexing the book. This is the first time we have worked together and I have enjoyed it very much.

Mary Gay Marchese, of Markzware (Markzware.com), who gave me permission to reprint their glossary of desktop publishing terms from the FlightCheck Professional user manual.

The people of PhotoSpin.com who so graciously have allowed me to use their photos and illustrations in this book. I had a lot of fun using them. Other photos and illustrations are from iStockPhoto.com as well as my own scans and artwork.

The Neat Company, which provided the photo of the NeatDesk scanner. **Viprofix Systems for Publishing**, which provided the photo of the Howtek drum scanner.

Brad Neal, one of the "car guys," who gave me the interview on the benefits of providing photorealistic vector artwork.

I also would like to thank all the following people who provided on-the-fly answers to technical questions: **Dov Issacs** of Adobe Systems for information on PDF printing. **Steve Werner**, **Chuck Weger**, **Jim Birkenseer**, **Peter Truskier**, and **David Zwang**.

Bob Levine, of TheInDesignGuy.com. Not only does Bob know all the minute details of InDesign, he knows it on both Windows and Mac. Thanks Bob for those late-night screen shots of the Windows platform.

Jay Nelson, of Design-Tools Monthly.com for help and guidance when it came to some of the features in QuarkXPress.

Jeff Gamet, of Design-Tools Monthly.com, who helped me get the FromDesignIntoPrint Web site and podcast up and running.

My sister, **Bonnie Cohen Gallet,** who took screen shots of applications on the Windows platform. Bonnie may not understand all that I do with computer graphics, but she knows a lot more about it than I know about the law. I hope this book will help her with her own projects.

And the following friends, students, and colleagues who form a world-wide support group of information, advice, and shoulders to lean on: **Terry DuPrât, Marcia Kagan, Diane Burns, Sharon Steuer, Mordy Golding, Scott Citron, David Blatner, Anne-Marie Concepcion, Gabriel Powell, Noha Edell, Russell Brown, Martinho da Gloria,** and **Barry Anderson.**

And a special thanks to **Pixel,** the cat, who gives me a never-ending supply of unconditional love.

And hey, let's be careful out there!

Sandee Cohen
sandee@FromDesignIntoPrint.com

Table of Contents

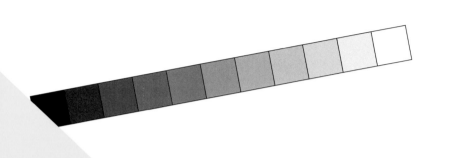

▶ START AT THE END

You can't plan a journey until you know where you're going.
Here's how to figure out your intended results.

"That's the effect of living backwards,"
the Queen said kindly,
"it always makes one a little giddy at first."

LEWIS CARROLL
THROUGH THE LOOKING GLASS

Know Where You're Going

1

Before you begin to create your printed project—before you type a headline, sketch an illustration, or take a photo, before you even turn on your computer—you have to know your final goal.

In this chapter we'll discuss the questions you need to ask before you start your project, and how to understand the answers.

What are the questions?

When you start a printed project, there are three important questions to ask before you start working:

1. What kind of project is it?

2. How much money can I spend?

3. When is it due?

The kind of project tells you the physical properties of the piece, such as general size, approximate number of pages, number of colors, etc. Is it a book? A brochure? An annual report? A single-page flyer? How are the pages held together? The physical properties will determine many factors in the production and printing of your work.

How much money you can spend lets you know your budget for the project. You won't be able to hire a famous photographer or print in full color if it's a low-budget project (of course, what's "low-budget" for one person may seem like a fortune to another). Whether the budget is high or low, you need to know your financial limitations so you can plan on how much to spend. (This also helps when grocery shopping or buying a car.)

The due date, or deadline, tells you when the project needs to be finished. The deadline can be in a year, a month, a week, or we-need-it-immediately! Some dates are flexible; some are very fixed. "We need it in the third quarter" is a flexible date; "We need it to hand out at the 3 p.m. meeting" is a fixed date. Once you know the final deadline, you can plan the due dates for other parts of the project so everything will be ready on time. For instance, if you do hire that famous photographer to take pictures for your piece, you will need to tell her when she has to send you the photos so you can incorporate them into the project; her deadline is earlier than your final deadline.

Sample schedule

The following shows a sample schedule for creating a single-page ad for a client.

ITEM	WK 1	WK 2	WK 3	WK 4
Client meeting to discuss the ad. Client brings previous ads and promotion material.	X			
Client provides copy for ad.	X			
Designer starts comps for two versions of the ad. (Note: If necessary, three versions may be presented to the client.)		X		
Send client PDF files of comps. Telephone call to discuss recommendation and approved comp.		X		
If necessary make revisions of comps and resend comp for final approval.		X		
Schedule photo shoot.		X		
First layout with placeholder art is sent to client for proofing.		X		
Photo shoot.			X	
Choose photo and start retouching.			X	
Add photos to layout and send PDF to client.			X	
Receive PDF comments from client and make corrections.			X	
Send final corrected PDF to client for approval.			X	
Send finished PDF to publication.				X

When to ask questions

If you are working for someone else, don't be afraid to ask questions. You don't look like a novice when you ask—you actually look pretty smart.

In addition to the three main questions above, you also need to ask—and answer—the following questions before you start on a project. Some of the answers you'll get from your client; some you'll have to figure out for yourself; some will come from other people, such as the manager of a print shop or the art director of a publication.

What kind of job is it?

Most people tell you the type of project you're going to work on when they give you the assignment. They say things like, "We need an advertisement to run in the paper announcing a sale." Or, "Would you design a menu for my new café?" If you're doing the work for yourself, you'll say something like, "I should create a flyer to hand out at the mall so people will know I'm open for business." In those cases you know immediately the type of job you're working on.

Sometimes people are a little vague as to what type of project they need. They might say, "I need something to publicize my bed-and-breakfast." Or you might say to yourself, "I sure would like to let people know we're going out of business next week." In those cases you and your client need to take a long time to talk and decide what type of job it is. You won't be able to make any further decisions until you've got this one answered.

Who's printing it?

There are a variety of ways to reproduce your work, from your office inkjet printer, a copy shop, or a small print shop, to a large, commercial press. The process you choose depends on your project. Because it's good to understand the advantages and disadvantages of each level of printing and exactly when to choose each one, we elaborate on this topic in Chapters 2 and 3. You should also understand process color (Chapter 9) and spot color printing (Chapter 10) before you make a firm decision on how to proceed with a big job.

Sending Jobs To Publications

What if you're not printing the job at all? It's possible that instead of creating a printed project, you're creating an advertisement that is going into a magazine or brochure. Or you might be sending a page that will be printed by your client on their own. In those cases you need to call the publication or the client's print shop to find out the details of the project.

What's the size of the paper?

This question may seem straightforward, but it can actually be a little tricky. Go get your morning newspaper and measure the size of a page. It's probably around 12 inches wide by 22 inches tall. (At least that's the size of *The New York Times*, which is the paper I have delivered each morning. *The Daily News* is a smaller paper.)

Now unfold the paper and measure it again. This second measurement is the actual size of the *piece of paper*. For *The Times*, this measurement is 24 by 22 inches. The first measurement was the size of the *page*.

If you are designing a brochure or a flyer that will be folded, then you need to know the size of the paper *before* folding. Then you can figure out the size of the individual pages *after* folding. This is a common mistake: We often confuse the page of text or graphics with the size of the paper it will be printed on.

How many pieces of paper?

Once you've decided what kind of job it is and what the paper size is, you need to know how many pieces of paper are necessary for the project. If you plan to reproduce the project on a laser printer or photocopier, you can print on both sides of the paper. For example, a report that has 20 letter-size pages (meaning 8 ½ x 11 inches) uses only 10 pieces of folded 11-x-17-inch paper (two letter-size pages fit on one sheet of 11-x-17-inch paper). And then only five sheets of paper if you print on both sides of the paper. However, if you're having your job professionally printed, you need to talk to the print shop about the final number of printed pieces of paper.

Working with signatures

If you're planning to create a multi-page document that will be produced on a printing press, such as a brochure, newsletter, annual report, or book, you need to check with the print shop about the total number of pages you think you'll have. Because projects like books and lengthy newsletters are printed in units called signatures (defined below), you may end up with extra, blank pages at the end of your piece if you don't plan carefully.

Books and newsletters that are printed at a professional printing establishment that uses big paper presses are not printed on individual sheets of paper that are the same size as those in the final product. These multi-page documents are printed on large sheets or rolls of paper with eight pages on one side and eight on the other side. This is called a "16-page signature" because when that one printed piece of paper is folded and trimmed, the result is 16 pages of the book held together at its folded edge. The folded set of pages is called the **signature**.

Signatures are bundles of papers grouped together to bind books, magazines, and other long documents. You can see the signatures in most hard cover books.

You have to think in **signature units**. If your signature unit is 16, then the number of pages in your project can be 16, 32, 48, 64, 80 and so on — any multiple of 16. If your signature is 8, the number of pages can be 8, 16, 24, 32, 40, 48, and so on.

So what happens if your final project is only 67 pages? With a 16-page signature unit, your options are either 64 pages—not enough pages—or 80 pages in which case you'll have 13 blank pages at the end of the book which is considered unacceptable by most publishers.

There are several ways to fix this: You can *add* 13 pages of copy and illustrations to fill up the blank pages. You can *cut* 3 pages of copy so the book fits into 64 pages. Or, if you are working for a large publishing house, you can *ask the printer* to switch to an 8-page signature and then add copy for only 5 extra pages (the next 8-page signature after 67 is 72). This is what Peachpit Press routinely does for many of my books.

You need to find out the signature unit before you do much work on a project destined for a printing press. You'd hate to discover that you have five blank pages at the end of a lengthy report, especially if you had told the client that the letter from the company president had to be cut because there wasn't room for it.

Understanding imposition

When you read a magazine or brochure, you read from page 1 to page 2 to page 3 and so on. This is also how a page layout program such as InDesign or QuarkXPress displays the pages. This display is called **reader's spreads**.

However, printed materials are not always printed in the same order that you read. Your print shop may tell you that the pages for a job need to be arranged in a certain order. Let's say you create an 8-page brochure, and each individual page is 8 ½-x-11 inches. The print shop will print two pages, side by side, on one 11-x-17-inch piece of paper. Then they print two different newsletter pages on the other side of the paper.

When pages are imposed, the order of the pages depends on the number of pages in each signature. Here the pages for an 8-page signature are assembled together.

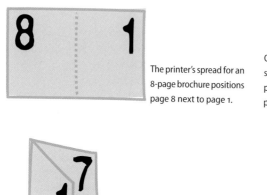

The printer's spread for an 8-page brochure positions page 8 next to page 1.

On the other side of the same piece of paper, the printer's spread positions page 2 next to page 7.

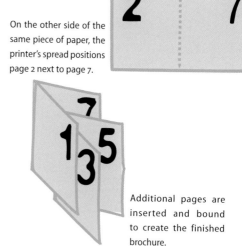

When this piece of pape is folded, the pages form the outside of the brochure.

Additional pages are inserted and bound to create the finished brochure.

To make sure these pages are in the correct order when the job is finished and folded, the print shop will arrange the pages in a special order called a **printer's spread**. For instance, in a typical 8-page brochure, page 1 is printed to the right of page 8, on one wide piece of paper. On the other side of that piece of paper, page 2 is printed next to page 7. Page 3 is printed next to page 6, and on its other side, the printer's spread is pages 4 and 5. When the brochure is bound together, the pages read in proper order. (If you want to see printer's spreads, take apart the pages of a catalog. You'll see how the pages are arranged next to each other. Or create the spread above with numbered pieces of paper.) The final position of the pages, set up in printer's spreads, is called **imposition**. (For more information on imposition, see Chapter 16.)

How many folds?

Look at your own newspaper: As you discovered, folding the *paper* changes the size of the individual *pages*. Each time you add a fold, you add more pages to the job.

Let's say you've decided to create a folded brochure to fit in a business envelope. It's a good idea to take a piece of paper and fold it up the way you want the finished project to look. (You can just scribble where you want the headline, the images, and the body copy to appear.)

If someone else will be printing the job, such as your local print shop, take this "mock-up" to make sure it can be printed as such. Some types of folds are tricky and can't be done by machine— they have to be folded by hand, which can be very costly. You don't want that cost to surprise you. You might have to rearrange your folding, depending on what the print shop suggests.

If your job requires creating lots of folded brochures and letters, you should invest in a copy of *A Field Guide to Folding* by Trish Witkowski. This 200-page paperback contains everything you need to know about folding paper, including what types of paper work best with which types of folded products.

How many copies?

The answer to "How many copies?" is pretty simple to figure out—it is how many finished pieces of the project you will have. The number of finished pieces is sometimes called the **print run**. The print run will often determine what kind of printing process you should choose.

For instance, if you only need 500 finished copies of a full-color page, it might cost $1,000 to have it printed at a commercial print shop, which means that each copy costs about $2 to produce. However, 500 copies can be printed on a color photocopier, which might cost only 40¢ a page, for a total cost of $200. You do the math! The copy shop wins on this one!

But let's say you need 10,000 copies of this same page. The copy shop might be able to bring down the cost per page to 30¢ each, for a total cost of $3,000, but at the commercial print shop those 10,000 copies may cost only $1,000 total. That's because once a job starts to run on a commercial printing press, there is very little difference between printing 500 copies or 10,000. So the more copies you print, the less each individual unit (each copy of the finished project) will cost. Suddenly the commercial print shop becomes a much better deal.

For the most part, copy shops are most economical for print runs under 500 pieces, and it is more affordable to use commercial print shops for anything over 10,000. So what about print runs in between? It depends on the job. Ask your local print shop what their estimate is. See Chapter 3 for more details on estimating these costs.

How many colors?

The question of color can be tricky. It's not about how many colors are on the page, but how many inks are needed to create those colors. For instance, look at the pages in a magazine such as *Time* or *Newsweek*. A single page might have red, blue, green, yellow, orange, purple, brown, black, and pink elements on the page. That doesn't mean the magazines were printed using all those colors. They were printed using only four colored inks (cyan, magenta, yellow, and black) that are mixed on the page to create many other colors. This is called **process printing** and is covered in Chapter 9.

However there are times when you might want to add just a single color such as gold or bright orange in addition to the black ink. This is called **spot color printing** and is covered in Chapter 10.

When you are deciding how many colors for a job, you are really deciding on how many inks. The more inks, the higher the cost.

The color of the paper doesn't count as a color! If you print your job using black ink on pink paper, it still counts as only one color because the print shop is only using one ink (black) on the press. The paper itself provides the other color.

Using any graphics?

A graphic is anything that isn't text. This doesn't include the little fancy rules between sections of a document or the little dingbat illustrations that are part of a font. For instance, the typeface I'm typing in right now includes these cute little dingbat glyphs: ▣, ▦, ◣, ⬛, ▸◂, and 🐾.

I don't consider these graphics because they are part of the typeface. I can insert them in my design simply by typing on the keyboard. I call that inserting a character, not a graphic.

An actual graphic can be a photograph, such as a picture of the corporate headquarters; or a drawing, such as a map showing the best route to the party; or a separate software file, such as a bar graph from a spreadsheet. You won't find these in a typeface.

A graphic can appear on a small section of the page or it can be a texture that covers the entire page.

A **photograph** may be scanned into the computer or transferred from a digital camera.

An **illustration** may be created using an illustration program such as Adobe Illustrator or page layout program like Adobe InDesign.

A **graph or pie chart** may be created in a spreadsheet or illustration program.

Examples of the types of graphics you might use in a project.

Once you realize your project will have graphics, you may need to reconsider some of the other questions in this chapter. For instance, if you are going to show photographs of the food served in a restaurant, you may not want to print those photos using only black ink—you may want to use color inks to make sure the food looks as delicious as possible.

You may also decide that the green ink you want to use really isn't appropriate if you have to include a photograph of the company president—black or brown might be a better choice.

Different types of graphics may also require different printing processes. You've probably noticed that a photograph looks much better when printed professionally compared to one reproduced on a desktop printer or photocopier. A simple line drawing, however, can be reproduced rather well using an ordinary desktop printer.

What kind of paper?

If you are printing your job using an ordinary desktop laser printer or going to a small copy shop, many of your paper questions will be easy to answer because only certain types of papers can be used in those printers or copiers. Those papers may be bought at your local stationery store or office supply shop, or you can order them from specialty paper catalogs. As soon as you choose to use a professional print shop to reproduce your job, there are other things to consider about the paper, some of which you may need to discuss with the print shop.

Paper color

Most paper is white. However, there are hundreds of different shades of white. Some whites are very warm, almost yellow; others are cool, almost blue or gray. Your print shop should be able to give you samples of different paper colors.

If you are using a desktop printer or photocopier, you can also choose between these different variations of white. Many companies use a plain, duller white paper for their ordinary print jobs because it tends to be less expensive, and then choose a brighter, more expensive white paper for special output.

Of course, you can also get paper in colors. Most copy shops and commercial presses have a wide variety of colors to choose from that will give more impact to flyers, invitations, and garage sale notices. However, keep in mind that most photographs don't look so good on colored papers—our eyes just aren't used to seeing the "whites" of a photograph as blue or pink.

Most professional printing starts with plain, white paper. Sometimes the entire paper is covered with ink so that it looks like the paper itself is a certain color. One way to determine the original color of the paper is to see if there is any white on the page or anywhere in a photograph. If there is white, then, almost certainly, that was the original color of the paper.

However, there are times when you will be printing onto a suface (technically called a **substrate**) that is not white. For instance, my favorite snacks come in little bags that have color printed on a silver substrate. Any white that is on the bag is actually a separate color ink that needs to be specified as a special color added to the document.

Paper coating

Papers are coated or uncoated, which refers to how smooth the surface of the paper feels. The degree of smoothness is created during the paper-making process.

Uncoated papers are rougher and tend to be porous (they soak up more ink). The paper used for newspapers and cheap catalogs is uncoated.

Coated papers are smooth and range from a rather dull coating to very glossy. They might be coated on only one side or on both. On coated papers, photographs and illustrations look sharp and crisp because the ink doesn't absorb into the paper.

Don't confuse coated paper with varnished or laminated paper. Varnishing or lamination is actually part of the printing process, where extra coatings of clear shellac or plastic are applied to add even more gloss to a paper. Go look at the boxes for most bars of soap. That surface is usually varnished to keep moisture from the product inside.

Paper finishes

A paper's finish is the texture or smoothness of the paper. An antique finish is a rough texture. Eggshell or vellum finishes are smoother. There are also specialty finishes made to simulate the look of fabrics, such as tweed or linen. Keep in mind that if you use a paper with a textured finish, your text might not look as clean or the illustrations may look a little rough because the ink has to bend up and down around the nooks and crannies of the finish.

Paper weight

Paper is graded according to its weight — which is usually expressed in terms of how much 500 sheets of the paper in its standard size weighs.

The typical bond paper for a laser printer or copy machine is listed as 24-pound; lighter bond paper is 20-pound.

Book paper is either coated or uncoated and can weigh between 30 and 110 pounds. Despite the name, book paper can be used for books, magazines, posters, flyers, or any job that doesn't need exceptional quality.

Text paper is the term used to describe a high-quality coated or uncoated paper used for better-quality printing. Annual reports, magazine inserts, and premium movie and theatre programs use text. Common weights of text papers are 70- or 80-pound.

Cover stock is a heavier-weight paper that usually matches the colors of certain book papers. Cover stock can be used for book covers, business cards, postcards, or presentation covers. Typical cover weights are 60, 65, 80, or 100.

As a general rule, the heavier the paper the more it costs. If you are going to mail your printed piece, take into consideration the weight of the paper because it might affect the postage you have to pay.

Other paper considerations

There are a few other features to consider when looking at paper.

Strength is how well the paper holds up under stress. Paper bags and envelopes need a high degree of strength.

Thickness is how thick the paper is. Thick papers don't have to weigh a lot. Some books are printed on very thick but lightweight paper, which makes the book look like it has more pages.

Brightness is how light reflects off the paper. Some papers contain fluorescents so they appear brighter. This makes the paper sparkle more, but can affect the color of printed images.

Opacity refers to how much the text or images printed on the other side of the page show through. If you are creating a book with lots of text and illustrations, make sure the opacity is not too low or your readers will be distracted by the images and text from the other side of the paper.

You may also want to consider using a **recycled paper** that comes from at least 30% of used papers.

What holds it together?

If you've got a printed project with more than one piece of paper, then you need to determine the binding for the job. *Binding* simply refers to the technique that holds the pages together.

Office bindings

If you are printing the project on a desktop printer or copier, you will most likely want to use one of the typical office bindings. Some of these bindings can be applied in your own office; others may need to be done by a local copy shop.

Three-ring binding uses three punched holes in the paper and a three-ring binder. The primary advantage of three-ring binding is that you can add or delete pages easily. Unfortunately, three-ring binding tends to remind people of their school days and screams amateur output.

Plastic comb binding uses a plastic insert with teeth that fit into rectangular holes in the paper. There are inexpensive kits that punch the holes in the paper as well as hold the teeth open. This makes it easier than manually trying to add or delete pages. There is usually a limit of 2 inches to the thickness of a plastic comb. Anything thicker tends to fall apart too easily.

Spiral binding uses a metal or plastic spiral that coils through many small holes on the side of the paper. Unlike the plastic comb, once you have bound the pages with the spiral, it is almost impossible to add more pages. (It's not too difficult to tear out pages, but you do have to delete the little strips of paper that collect inside the spiral.)

Wir-O binding is similar to spiral binding, but instead of a single spiral, two wire teeth fit into rectangular holes in the paper. Wir-O is sturdier than spiral binding but also makes it difficult to add pages to the document.

Velo binding uses two plastic strips on either side of the document. The strips are held together with plastic pins and bound together with heat. Velo-bound documents cannot be unbound without destroying the strips and pins.

Fastback binding uses a cloth or paper strip wrapped around the spine of the pages and then glued in position. Fastback is the most professional-appearing binding in an office environment, but the pages can fall out if the booklet is used a lot.

Saddle-stitch binding uses two or more staples inserted right at the fold of the paper. The pages of the document need to be printed on both sides of the paper in the correct position for final binding. This type of imposition is best handled by a professional copy shop or office document center.

Professional bindings

A print shop will ask what type of binding you want. They may also suggest one type over another depending on the number of pages you will need to hold together. Below are descriptions of the types of bindings typically used by professional print shops. (Some of these bindings are similar to the office bindings described in the previous section.) Some print shops do their own binding and finishing; many send the printed job to a separate company that binds and finishes it.

Spiral binding uses a metal or plastic spiral that coils through holes at the side of the paper.

Wir-O binding is similar to spiral binding, but is sturdier.

Saddle-stitch binding uses two or more staples inserted in the fold to hold both the cover and the pages.

Side-stitch binding combines all the signatures and the cover and stitches them together with staples on the outside of the book cover.

Perfect binding gathers all the signatures together. The spine is then ground to create a flat edge, and a paper cover is glued around the spine. Most magazines are bound this way.

Case binding sews the individual signatures together and glues them to a gauze strip, then affixes end papers with glue and attaches them onto hard covers. This is the most common form of binding for hardcover books.

Sewn-and-glued binding sews the signatures together and then glues them to a cover as in perfect binding. (This book has been bound using sewn-and-glued binding.)

Lay-flat binding gathers all the signatures together and grinds the spine as in perfect binding. The cover is then glued to the book at each side of the spine, which allows the pages of the book to lay flat when opened. However, pages tend to fly out of this type of binding if the spine of the book is opened too far.

Project preparation list

Copy the following table. Then fill out each of the categories before you start any project. I've left some space for you to add your own items. You can also go to: http://www.peachpit.com/designintoprint and download an interactive PDF file of these pages. You can use this file to organize your project before you start work.

BRIEF DESCRIPTION OF THE PROJECT	
What are the deadlines?	
When is the first draft due to the client?	
When is the second draft due to the client?	
When is the final project due at the print shop or publication?	
When is the job due for binding?	
PROJECT BUDGET	
Budget for printing	
Budget for photography or illustrations	
Budget for other expenses	
JOB DETAILS	
Paper size	
Page size	
Number of pages	
Number of colors	
Number of folds	

Signature units	
Graphics	
Number of final copies	
Paper description	
Paper coating	
Paper finish	
Paper weight (important for postage costs)	
Special paper considerations	
BINDING	
Type of binding	
Print information	
Laser or copier printing	
Type of printer/copier	
INFORMATION ABOUT COPY SHOP OR PRINT SHOP	
Name	
Address	
Phone	
Contact person	
Email or Web site information	
PUBLICATION	
Name of publication	
Ad to be shipped to	

Issue date	
Ad size	
Deadline at publication	
Deadline extension	
Publication sales rep	
Production contact	
Email or Web site information	
Job notes	
OTHER	

Desktop Printing

2

Instead of taking their print or design jobs to a print shop, many people are able to output the jobs right from their own computer desktop by using one of the wide variety of available desktop printers. But what makes a printer a "desktop" printer? Well, some printers are actually as big as a room and would obviously crush your desk. But others are small enough to tuck into a briefcase and take on the road. Some print copies that are almost identical to photographs. Others collate and staple like office copiers.

Most people consider a desktop printer to be any **output device** that can be hooked up to a personal computer. There's no official definition of a desktop printer, so there are many different types of printers you can use in-house to reproduce your project.

You can also take your computer files to a local copy shop to **output** (print out your files) on the printers that are connected to their computers. This is not the same as having your project professionally printed—it simply means you're using someone else's desktop printer.

Each type of printer gives different types of results. Some printers are better at photos; others are better at text; others may require special paper to print at their highest quality. No matter what type of printer you finally use, you should know what type you expect to use before you do too much work on the job. This will help prevent problems later on.

General printer considerations

Here's a list of the important factors you should consider when deciding which sort of printer you should use for different types of projects.

Resolution

Resolution is an extremely important part of all desktop publishing. In addition to setting the resolution for printing, you need to set the resolution for digital cameras, scanners, and creating artwork. We'll discuss those other aspects of resolution, but for this chapter, let's look at how resolution applies to printing.

Resolution *as it applies to printing* has to do with the size of the dots that make up the images of the printed piece. This resolution is usually expressed as **dots per inch** or DPI. The more dots per inch, the higher the resolution and the better the quality. So a printer that prints at 1200 DPI is higher quality than one that prints at 600 DPI.

One way to understand resolution for both printing and for digital images is to think about making a mosaic tile floor design. If you use tiles the size of a half dollar, you can't create many details. But if you use tiles the size of a quarter, you can create more details, and with tiles the size of a dime, you can create quite a detailed design.

In printing devices (both desktop and high-end), the size of the dot changes in relation to the number of dots per inch. A printer with a DPI of 600 has a certain size dot. A printer with a DPI of 1200 has a smaller dot. And a printer with a DPI of 2400 has an even smaller dot. This means that graphics output from a higher resolution printer (more and smaller dots) will produce more detailed artwork.

DPI or PPI?

Resolution is also used to describe the details in an image that comes out of a digital camera or a scanned image. This type of resolution is expressed as **pixels per inch**. Try to remember the difference: dots per inch (**DPI**) is for printing; pixels per inch (**PPI**) is for digital images.

Paper size

Paper size is simple: It's the size of the paper that the desktop printer uses. Some printers can only use paper up to 8½ x 11 inches in size. Other printers can use paper up to 11 x 17 inches. Some printers have multiple paper trays so you can switch from one size of paper to another quickly.

It's important to know what size of paper you're going to use so you can set up your page margins and artwork correctly, and make sure there's a desktop printer that can accommodate the size of paper you need.

Print area

The actual **print area**, the space in which the printer can apply ink or toner, is usually smaller than the physical size of the paper. This is because the printer needs some white space around the edge of the paper where the ink won't hit. If the printed image went right up to the edge of the paper, some of the ink could extend outside the paper and would fall inside the printer and make a mess.

An example of a printer that prints with white space around the image.

An example of a printer that prints right up to the edge of the paper.

A few desktop printers can print **edge-to-edge** which means they can apply ink or toner right up to the edge of the paper. So what do you do if you want to print to the edge of the paper but you don't have an edge-to-edge printer?

Most people print onto a larger piece of paper, and then trim the larger piece to the correct size. You might even extend or **bleed** the background image so it's larger than the final trim size; that way even if you don't trim the edges exactly straight, you won't see white gaps on the sides of the paper.

Speed

Another important consideration for working with desktop printers is their **speed**, or how many **pages per minute** (ppm) the printer can output. Desktop printers may have two different speeds, one for color and another for black. Some printers output their pages at the zippy rate of 45 pages per minute for plain black text. Others, especially those that add color to the page, crawl along at a lethargic 8 ppm.

Consider a printer that outputs in color at just 10 pages per minute. Printing 100 copies of a 20-page document could take more than three hours! Given that information, do you *really* want to apply red to all the page numbers? In many cases the added color might not justify the additional printing time.

Paper handling

Paper handling refers to features such as mixing different paper stocks in a single print run, collating multiple pages into a single document, stapling, and other finishing features. You should consider whether you need those types of features in your printer. The printers that provide these finishing features are rather large and are usually called **workgroup printers**, not desktop printers. Because I work out of my dining room, space is at a premium, so I do my own mixing of paper stocks and stapling.

Cost of goods

Cost of goods is accountant-type language for how much it costs to make copies after you've bought the desktop printer. There are two important aspects to the cost of goods for printers: the paper and the ink or toner.

Initial Speed

The speed of a printer doesn't count the initial time it takes to process a page. So you might see a print manufacturer list its printer as 30 PPM (pages per minute), with a **first print speed** of 6 seconds. This means that once the initial page has been processed in 6 seconds, it will take about 4.5 seconds to print the additional 9 copies of that page.

Most office reports are printed on plain bond paper. This type of paper costs much less than photographic-quality papers that are used for family photos.

So which paper should you use? There's no reason why you can't print a photograph on bond paper. The image just won't look as vivid as if it had been printed onto photographic paper.

There's also no reason why you can't print a resume or page from a report on photographic paper. It costs a bit more, but if you want your picture on your resume, it may be worth it.

Another cost of goods is the price of the ink or toner—the ink cartridges for an inkjet printer or the toner cartridges for a laser printer. The printer manufacturers will state that their cartridges last for a certain number of pages, but they're referring to text pages. If you're printing photographs or large, dense areas of color, a cartridge may empty in less than half the time expected.

With printers that use special papers and have high ink costs, you may find that doing the work in-house is not economical, especially for large print runs.

A Printer Is a Printer Is a Printer?

Try to be clear when you talk about "printers." Some people use the term *printer* for the machine that prints your documents. They may also send their jobs to the *printer*. That's the business that does the printing. They may also refer to the man who does the printing (usually with ink-stained fingers) as the *printer*. When I teach, I use the following terms to keep things clear. The **printing machine** is the mechanical beast that makes the copies. The **print shop** is the business that owns that mechanical beast. The **print shop person** is the guy or gal who operates the mechanical beast.

Types of printers

Most people are familiar with the inexpensive inkjet printers they use to print up a few copies of memos, resumes, or reports. But there are many different types of inkjet printers as well as other types of printing machines. The following chart can help you choose the right type of printer for your job.

TYPE OF PRINTER	ADVANTAGES	DISADVANTAGES
Inexpensive office inkjet printer	Economical for most office jobs.	Slow, expensive for large print runs.
High-end inkjet such as Iris® printers	Print oversized documents onto a wide variety of materials.	Expensive to purchase and maintain.
Laser printer	Excellent print quality, fast, can be networked with many users. Black-and-white output is very inexpensive.	Lower quality for photographs. Color laser printers are expensive compared to inkjet machines.
Imagesetters	Fine quality output onto film or photographic paper. This output can be used to make the plates for offset printing.	Extremely expensive to own and maintain. Are found almost exclusively in professional print shops.
Dye-sub printers	Extremely fine quality output that is as good as an original photograph.	Expensive to own and maintain. Mostly found in specialty print shops.
Film recorders	Print directly onto film. Can be used to convert files into 35 mm slides.	Expensive to own and maintain. Mostly found in specialty print shops.

Specialty printers

Yes, there are still other types of printers. For instance, there are **film recorders** that print directly onto film—you can turn an electronic presentation into ordinary 35 mm slides that can be used in slide presentations. There are also **sign plotters** that create oversized graphics, architectural prints, or lettering for signs and displays. If you need this type of output regularly, buy one of these types of printers to use in-house; otherwise, you'll want to find a copy shop or printer that can output your files for you. See Chapter 16 on sending files for output to outside print shops.

Summary

There are many different factors to consider when purchasing a printer. Some deal with the quality of the output while others deal with speed of printing and cost of goods.

One thing to remember, however, is you don't need a very expensive printer in your own office if most of your work will actually be output by an outside print shop or copy shop.

Printer quiz

The following quiz lists different types of projects that need to be printed. Choose the best printer for each project. Explain any adjustments you might make. There may be more than one correct answer for each project. Answers follow the quiz.

Project #1

You need 8 copies of a 10-page report to present to the client to show how much money you've made for them. The report has quite a few graphs that use colors to show how much money your clients have earned. Which printer should you use?

A. Inkjet onto bond paper; B. Inkjet onto photographic paper; C. Black-and-white laser printer; D. Other

Project #2

You need the same report in project #1 sent to 250 potential clients to show them what a good company you are. Which should you use?

A. Inkjet onto bond paper; B. Inkjet onto photographic paper; C. Professional copy shop; D. Black-and-white laser printer

Project #3

You have 20 photographs and artist's watercolor drawings of what your new corporate headquarters will look like. You need to print them up to show them to the board of directors to approve the project. Which should you use?

A. Inkjet onto bond paper; B. Inkjet onto photographic paper; C. Professional copy shop; D. Black-and-white laser printer

Project #4

You want to send in a printout of an ad for your company to the local newspaper. How should it be printed?

A. Inkjet onto bond paper; B. Imagesetter; C. Professional copy shop; D. Black-and-white laser printer

Project #5

You have a two-page press release with text about your company that needs to get to 50 magazine editors. What type of printer should you use?

A. Inkjet onto bond paper; B. Inkjet onto photographic paper; C. Professional copy shop; D. Black-and-white laser printer

Project #6

The same press release as in project #5 but with a photograph of the new corporate headquarters needs to get to 50 magazine editors. Which types of printers should you use?

A. Color inkjet for the whole project; B. Black-and-white laser for the whole job; C. Black-and-white laser for the text/color inkjet for the photographs; D. Professional copy shop

Project #7

You want to put up a banner across the front of your store with the words "Grand Opening Sale." How should it be printed?

A. On an office printer; B. At a copy shop; C. On a sign plotter.

Project #8

You have 10 new package designs for your products. You need to put those designs up on the wall of the boardroom for the directors to evaluate.

A. Color inkjet; B. Iris printer; C. Dye-sub printer; D. Black-and-white laser printer.

Printer quiz answers

Project #1

Answer A: The inkjet printer will give you the color that you need for the charts. You don't need more than the bond paper, however. The charts don't need photographic paper to look good.

Project #2

Answer C: 250 copies of the report are too many to tie up your inkjet printer and will cost too much in ink and paper. Get the job done by a professional copy shop and save yourself the time and materials.

Project #3

Answer B or C: The inkjet onto photographic paper is a good choice, but if you've got millions of dollars riding on the board's decision, go to a professional copy shop. They'll make sure the printing looks good. (And they may even mount the prints on stiff boards for presentation.)

Project #4

Answer B: The imagesetter device has the high resolution you need to make sure your ad looks perfect. Of course, you can also ask the newspaper if they will accept an electronic version of the ad. That way you won't need to print anything.

Project #5

Answer A or D: Both the inkjet onto bond paper or the black-and-white laser printer will be fine. However, the laser printer looks a little crisper on the paper and won't smudge if it gets wet. If you want the job to look its best, go with the laser printer.

Project #6

Answer C: The black-and-white laser with the color inkjet will be fine. And with only 50 copies needed, you don't have to worry too much about the cost of materials.

Project #7

Answer C: A sign plotter or some other oversized printing device is the best way to get a very large banner. Ask your local copy shop or print shop if they have this type of equipment.

Project #8

Answer A, B, or C: You want the project to look its best. If the package designs are simple graphs, the inkjet printer will be fine. If they have photos, you should consider an Iris or dye-sub printer.

The Basics of
Commercial Printing

Printing is simply the reproduction of images in quantity. Creating one image, such as a painting or a drawing, is art; reproducing an image into many copies is printing.

Printing has been around for centuries. Although Gutenberg created the first moveable type printing press in 1440, the Chinese had block printing as early as 200 AD. The speedier rotary press came in the middle of the 19th century.

Ever since the Industrial Revolution, office workers have needed to quickly make many copies of their typewritten and illustrated documents. Most of these techniques used versions of photography, stencils, or carbon papers. Photography required messy liquids and expensive equipment. Stencils had a limited number of copies that could be created. And carbon paper made a very poor impression as the number of copies increased. The invention of xerography, (introduced by the Haloid company in 1959, later known as Xerox) created a quicker, cleaner way to duplicate documents. Xerography machines were the parents of computer printers as well as digital printing presses.

Today the distinction between printing and duplicating is more a question of semantics. As a general rule I call **printing** any process that puts different colors of ink separately on a surface. For instance, a magazine is printed by four different plates of ink. I call something **digitally printed** or **duplicated** when all the color is applied during a single pass through a machine.

Print shops, copy shops, and online printing

It can be confusing choosing which type of place you should go to to duplicate or print your layouts.

Copy shops

For many small businesses, professional copy shops provide all the services one might find in corporate duplicating departments.

Most copy shops have extremely sophisticated equipment, including high-speed copiers that can collate and staple large jobs in a very short time. They also have color copiers, large-format copiers, and limited binding services. But they rarely provide true printing services.

Some copy shops let you rent time at their computers to print your work using their desktop printers. You can also bring your files in for output on their high-end printers. (I've got a great copy shop three blocks from my house where I can duplicate my files on their fancy color printers.)

Small print shops

Small print shops, or printing press operations, specialize in jobs for local businesses such as newsletters, brochures, invitations, stationery, labels, envelopes, menus, business forms, business cards, stickers, catalogs, and so on. In addition to traditional printing, they may also provide digital and photocopy services.

The main benefit of working with a local print shop as opposed to a national commercial print shop (covered in the following section) is that it's very easy to check on the status of your work and make adjustments, by looking at an advance copy that's called a **proof**. You can also save money on shipping costs when you deal with a local print shop.

Copy Shop Or Print Shop?

It may be hard to tell if a business is a copy shop or a print shop. In my neighborhood we have a copy shop where all the college students get their papers duplicated. But this same place does simple offset printing for business cards and newsletters.

So, which is it, copy shop or print shop? It really doesn't matter what the place is called as long as you understand what it does.

National commercial print shops

National print shops are the mammoth printing companies that reproduce national magazines, books, packaging, sales brochures, or annual reports for major corporations all over the world. Most of these companies offer only traditional or digital printing on large presses.

In order to work with these organizations, you should be prepared to allot extra time to ship your files and proofs back and forth between you and the main print headquarters. Occasionally a print shop will ask a designer or production manager to visit the print shop on a press check. A **press check** means that you'll be shown samples of the job at different stages of the printing. You can then approve the print or ask the shop to adjust the colors.

Using a national shop may cost you extra in shipping charges or the cost of traveling to the press check.

Online print services

Books, clothes, and music aren't the only things you can buy on the Web. Many print shops have Web sites where you can send in orders for business cards, postcards, brochures, and other print jobs.

Some of these online services offer barebones services without the opportunity to see proofs. Others offer Web images that you can use to proof your work. Still others will send you a hard-copy proof that you can approve or make changes to.

I like online printing services for jobs where I'm not concerned about matching exact colors. My business cards as well as some promotional postcards have been printed using online services.

However, I wouldn't want to use one of these services if I were concerned about the type of paper or matching colors. For example, suppose you were the designer working on a brochure for a winery. You wouldn't want the image of a glass of bordeaux to end up looking like a burgundy. In that situation, I would choose a press that would let me proof the job as it was coming off the press.

To copy or to print?

A Simple Guide for Printing: Good, Fast, or Cheap?
Pick any two.

As copiers, especially color copiers, become more sophisticated, it becomes harder to choose between traditional printing and photocopying. The decision is not an easy one. There are many different criteria you have to consider; here are some of the guidelines.

CONSIDERATION	PRINTING PRESS	COPY MACHINE
QUALITY		
There is a clear difference between the look of a photocopied document and a real printed piece. If you need high-quality, go to press.	Solid areas of color tend to look more uniform. Printed pieces usually start from high-resolution imagesetters so the type and lines are cleaner and crisper.	Most photocopiers can't handle photographs or subtle images well. The toner from a copier can flake off the paper, unlike the ink from a printing press.
ECONOMY		
The economics of photocopying and printing depend mostly on how many copies you need.	Printing is more economical for jobs over 1,000 units. Digital printing is excellent for jobs between 500 and 1,000 units.	Photocopying usually has a fixed cost—each unit costs the same whether you make 10 or 100 copies. Photocopying is best for jobs under 500 copies.
SPEED		
There is a great difference in how quickly a job can be finished.	Printing takes longer to get ready for the press. Digital printing, however, is much faster than traditional printing.	Photocopying is ready to start as soon as you bring in the material.
MATERIALS		
Photocopiers are very limited as to the kinds of papers or other materials they can print onto. A printing press has far more choices.	You can print onto plastic, vinyl, or many other materials for special effects.	Photocopiers do not print well onto textured papers, and not at all onto plastic or vinyl.

Different printing processes

Choosing the specific type of printing process for your job is not something you have to do yourself. Even professional designers with years of experience may not know the difference between **offset lithography** and **gravure printing**. Once you've decided to use a commercial printer, your safest decision is to go to the print shop and ask its operators what they think is best for your job.

Here are descriptions of most of the printing processes and why your print shop might suggest using one over another. Understanding these options will help you decide on the best process.

Letterpress

Letterpress is the oldest form of printing. Letterpress starts with a piece of metal, called a **plate**, that contains the image to be printed. Or instead of one solid plate, there might be a collection of smaller pieces, such as individual letters or illustrations made of metal, or perhaps large letters made of wood, grouped together into a block. The area that prints is raised above the non-printing areas. Inked rollers run across the plate, transferring the ink to the raised surfaces only. The paper is then pressed onto the inked plate.

The images created by letterpress printing can be crisp and sharp. It's a wonderfully tactile form of printing because on the finished piece you can feel the indentations in the paper made by the metal characters. However, if you look closely at the edges of letterpress printing you might see a slight area around the edge of the image where the ink is a bit heavier.

Although it once was the most popular (and for many years, the only) form of printing, letterpress is rarely used today for commercial work. It has evolved into a beautiful art form practiced by passionate typographers and printers working on hand-bound and limited editions.

Flexography

Flexography uses the same principle as letterpress in that the printing image is raised above the rest of the area. However, as the name suggests, flexography uses flexible rubber or polymer plates that can conform to uneven surfaces. This has made flexography an extremely useful process. It was originally used for printing on paper bags, corrugated boxes, and other packaging material, but its fast-drying inks make it ideal for printing on slick surfaces such as plastic grocery bags, milk cartons, and even shower curtains. As the technology behind flexography has improved, it has been used to print newspaper and magazines.

Recently flexographic printing has become even more popular because of its environmental considerations: Unlike the oil-based inks used in other types of printing, flexography uses environmentally friendly water-based inks or non-solvent inks.

Gravure

Gravure printing uses a method that is the reverse of letterpress. In gravure printing the image area is **recessed** into a copper cylinder plate. Ink is held inside the recesses of the plate. The paper quickly and lightly presses against the plate and the ink is transferred from the recesses onto the paper.

Gravure printing is excellent for photographs. However, the time and expense needed to create the cylinder makes it economical only for long-run jobs. Many catalogs, magazines, and newspaper supplements are printed using gravure printing presses.

Printing Trivia

When gravure plates are printed onto paper that spools off of big rolls, the process is called **rotogravure**. This is the rotogravure mentioned in Irving Berlin's song "Easter Parade." The lyric goes: "The photographers will snap us, and you'll find that you're in the *rotogravure*."
What he was saying is that he and his lady friend would be featured in the photo section of the newspaper.

Steel-die engraving

Steel-die engraving is a type of gravure printing where slightly wet paper is forced against the recessed plate. The pressure against the plate forces the ink from the recessed areas onto the paper. This pressure also raises the image slightly, which gives the characteristic look and feel of engraved invitations, wedding announcements, stock certificates, letterheads, and money.

Thermography

The **thermography** process creates an even greater raised effect than engraving but it's faster and cheaper, which is why it's also called "poor man's engraving." In thermography, special powder is added to the wet ink on the surface of the paper. The combination of ink and powder is then passed under heat, hence the name *thermo*graphy. Under the heat, the powder and ink are fused together and they swell to create a raised effect.

Many shops that print stationery and business cards can print using thermography, if you request it. I particularly like the old-time feel of thermography for business cards, but it's limited to artwork without screens or photographs. *(For more about screens see Chapter 6.)*

Offset lithography

This is the most popular of the different printing processes and is sometimes just called **offset**, **lithography**, or **litho offset**. **Offset lithography** uses a chemical process in which the image areas of the metal plate are made to attract grease or oil, and the non-image areas of the plate are made to attract water. Water rollers coat the non-image areas with water; ink rollers coat the image areas with oil-based ink. Because water and oil don't mix, the image areas keep the ink in place. The ink is then transferred, or offset, onto the paper.

Most small print shops use offset printing presses as well as the large commercial operations. Offset printed pieces are recognized by a smooth edge to the text and images, and there is no indentation of the paper or raising of the ink.

Screen printing

I still call this by its older name, **silkscreen printing** from when I went to summer camp and did my own silkscreen printing. **Screen printing** uses a fine mesh screen made from stainless steel or from fabric such as silk or polyester. I used a silk cloth. The screen is mounted on a frame that sits on top of the material that's to be printed. Areas of the screen that are not to be printed are blocked out as with a stencil.

I cut my own stencils in summer camp by hand which meant they had to be very simple. Today there are photographic and chemical processes that make screen printing a lot faster and more precise. A squeegee is used to force ink through the open areas of the stencil onto the material.

The big advantage to screen printing is that you can print any surface, which makes it extremely useful for banners, posters, t-shirts, CDs, etc. Back in my summer camp, I created a very primitive t-shirt and a headscarf.

An example of how a squeegee presses ink into a screen for screen printing.

You should talk to the shop that will be printing your job before you spend too much time working on graphics for screen printing. For instance, ordinary screen printing is not recommended for printing photographs or small text because those graphics lose detail as the ink passes through the mesh screen. You also may need to specify colors differently when preparing graphics for screen printing.

If you want to print photographic artwork onto fabrics, there are special photo emulsion papers that allow screen printers to transfer intricate graphics or photographs onto screens for printing. When screen printing is used to create fine art prints, it's called **serigraphy**.

Collotype or screenless printing

All the previously mentioned forms of printing use **halftone screens** to reproduce photographs, illustrations, or tints of color. These screens are series of dots in varying sizes that make image areas appear darker or lighter. (*For more information on halftone screens, see Chapter 6.*) But **collotype printing** uses special photo-gelatin plates to print without halftone dots so the images look more like photography. This screenless printing provides better control over tints, blends, and the midtones of photographs. Collotype is expensive and slow, so it's used for limited print runs such as specialized posters.

Digital color printing

One of the newest advances in printing technology is **digital printing**. Some digital printers use the same technology as photocopiers; others use combinations of lasers that make the plates and conventional offset printing.

Digital printing is ideal for short runs of full-color jobs that need to be printed quickly. Digital printing also makes it easy to change elements of the job. For instance, you could have one address in a brochure that goes to the south and another address for the north. But digital printing tends to be priced like photocopying (it doesn't get cheaper per unit when you make more), so for large runs it may be more economical to use traditional printing.

Direct-to-plate

Direct-to-plate is also called **computer-to-plate** (**CTP**). CTP isn't really a printing process—it's a way of shortcutting the traditional printing process.

Most printing involves making some kind of "plate" onto which text and graphics are depicted. Ink is applied to the plate, which is transferred from the plate to the paper during the printing process. This plate can be made of metal, stiff board, rubber, or other materials. But first, to make the plate, the operator needs to expose pages onto negative film. In the direct-to-plate method, he can skip the film step. Instead of creating film with an imagesetter, the direct-to-plate printer creates the actual plate used for printing.

The main advantages of direct-to-plate printing are the savings in film cost and time. However, high-end color jobs don't always lend themselves to direct-to-plate printing.

How to find a print shop

If you live in a large city like New York, it's not hard to find a local print shop. Most are listed in the phone book. Also, use Google or an online search engine to find something in your neighborhood. Call them up and ask to speak to a sales representative, and make an appointment to discuss your project. If you are in the suburbs, you may have to drive to the nearest city to find a local print shop.

As mentioned before, you should talk to the print shop that will be printing your job before you do too much work. The sales representative will be glad to make suggestions and will show you different paper samples, ink colors, or binding options. This will make it easier for you to complete the project.

What to bring to the appointment

Be prepared for your appointment with the printing sales representative. Here are some of the things you should know about your project before you meet with the printer.

- ▶ **How many finished pieces do you need?** Do you need some now and others later? You might ask if it's possible for the shop to print all the copies now and store the ones you'll need later. It might cost you some storage fees, but it could be cheaper than printing the job in two separate print runs.

- ▶ **When do you need the project completed?** Is this a flexible date? Printers hate to have their machines left idling. You might be able to save money if you can tell the print shop you're willing to wait for a time when it's not busy.

- ▶ **How will you get your files to the print shop?** Will you send your files electronically via an Internet connection, or will you send a disk with the documents? If you're sending a disk, make sure the print shop can open your disk on their computer.

- ▶ **What type of files do they want you to send?** The print shop must be able to open and print your files, so make sure that the print shop uses or has access to the same software you used to create your document. Some inexpensive home-publishing software or word processing programs are not common to commercial print shops. The print shop may ask you to save your job as a PDF file. This makes it easier for them to open and print your file. (See Chapter 17 for a complete discussion on working with PDF files.)

▶ **Does your job require any special colors?** For instance, do you need a certain color to match a client's logo? Or do you want colors to look like gold or silver? Explain any special color requirements up front.

▶ **Describe the project.** There are many variables to a print job that your print shop will consider that may not cross your mind. For instance, if it's a simple flyer that needs to be mailed, the print shop may suggest a certain weight of paper that won't be too expensive to mail. However, if it's a flyer that needs to be handed out, heavier paper may be advised.

▶ **Know your budget.** If the price quoted for the job seems too high, ask if there are ways the print shop can lower costs, such as using different paper, fewer colors, fewer copies, etc.

Printing on a budget

Professional printing doesn't have to cost a lot. Here are some choices that can help you save money as you design your project.

▶ One-color printing costs the least. However, that one color doesn't have to be plain black. And the paper doesn't have to be white.

▶ If you do use a color other than black, the print shop may charge a small fee to clean the black ink off the press before they start your job.

▶ Two-color printing costs more than one color, but less than four colors.

▶ Images or colors that "bleed" off the edge of the paper cost more to print. Setting a whitespace around the border of the design can reduce costs.

▶ Printing full-color on one side of the paper and one color on the other can save money.

▶ Letting the print shop substitute less-expensive paper or leftover paper from someone else's job can sometimes save money.

▶ Look for print shops that advertise on the Internet, which are probably out-of-town. Many of these will take your electronic files and print them together with other jobs. You won't be able to proof individual stages of the job, but you will save money.

Commercial printing projects

These are just some projects to get you thinking and looking at different types of printing. There are no right or wrong answers.

Project #1

Collect delivery or take-out menus from various local restaurants.

▶ Can you tell which ones were printed on photocopiers or desktop printers?

▶ Can you tell which ones were printed using offset or professional printing?

▶ See if you can find any take-out menus printed in full color; if not, why not?

Project #2

Find a local stationery store that will print wedding invitations. Ask to see some samples of the work.

▶ Can you tell if they're engraved or not? (This is something that's easier to feel than to see.)

Project #3

If the same store as in Project 2 also prints business cards or stationery, ask to see samples.

▶ Can you tell if they use engraving or thermography? If they have samples of both, which looks better?

Project #4

If you have a collection of business cards from various clients, contacts, etc., take them out and sort them into stacks:

▶ Find all the cards printed on copy machines or laser printers. How much of the toner is still on the cards?

▶ Find all the cards printed with thermography. How much of that printing is still on the cards?

▶ Feel the differences in the card papers. Are some heavier than the others? Are some different shades of white? Are some covered with a coating that makes it hard to write notes on the card?

Project #5

Look at the business cards you collected in Project 4. Is there a card that you really like the way it looks and feels? Call up the person on the card and ask where they got their card printed; it's good to keep track of print shops whose work you like and whose work you don't like.

Project #6

Look at the different types of printing in different magazines. Try to find the same ad printed on the *cover* of one magazine and on the *inside pages* of another. Or an ad that runs across the cover to the inside page. Is there any difference? Can you tell why there might be a difference?

Project #7

Go into your clothes drawers and look at any promotional and souvenir t-shirts you may have. Or go to a tourist area in your town and look at the shirts there.

▶ How were the shirts printed?

▶ How big is the type?

▶ Are there any photographs?

Project #8

Look at the yellow pages of your phone book.

▶ What color is most of the text?

▶ Are there photographs in the ads?

▶ How do those photographs look on colored paper?

▶ Are there any ads that have a white background? How do you think that white area was created?

▶ WHAT IS THE COMPUTER DOING?

If you're going to work with a computer to create your design and printing projects, you need to understand what's going on inside the computer and the software applications. In this section we'll look at what you need to know about how the computer is working with your files.

"I really must get a thinner pencil. I can't manage this one a bit: it writes all manner of things that I don't intend—"

LEWIS CARROLL
THROUGH THE LOOKING GLASS

Understanding the Types of Computer Applications

You can't buy oranges in a hardware store. It doesn't matter how diligently or how long you search. Hardware stores don't sell oranges. That's just not what they do.

It's the same with software programs. You can't make applications do things that they were never intended to do.

The difference between computer applications and hardware stores is that the people who run the hardware store will tell you they don't sell oranges. But when you're all alone working in front of your computer, there's no one there to tell you that a certain application can't do what you want it to.

Worse, it may look like the application can do what you want, but you won't find out till later that you wasted hours and hours of work using the wrong type of program.

This chapter is a guide to choosing the right types of applications, or programs, to do different jobs.

Choose your software

Computers are very limited machines when you first take them out of the box. They are one of the few tools that have no specific function—a computer can't do anything all by itself. Well, I guess a tower computer could be a doorstop and a laptop could be a cafeteria tray. But you have to add software applications to a computer to make it truly useful.

So first you buy the computer, then you add applications for creating graphics, page layouts, etc., and *then* you have a desktop publishing tool. But even if you have the right tool, you can still use it the wrong way.

Let's look at the various applications (also known as "programs") you will come across and what they are best used for—and not used for.

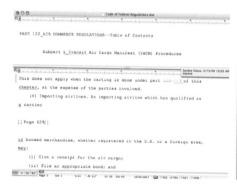 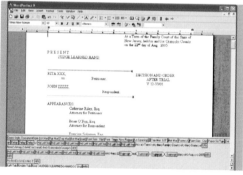

Microsoft Word (left) and WordPerfect (right) are two popular word processing applications.

Word processing applications

A word processing application, such as Microsoft Word or Corel WordPerfect, is very good at working with basic text. If you want to type fast, check your spelling and grammar, automate repetitive typing tasks, create outlines, track changes to the text, write reports with footnotes, make and organize tables of data, and print to desktop printers, then you should choose a word processor as your application.

What word processing applications are *not* good at is working with colors or creating high-end graphics. The drawing features found in word processors should be used only to create artwork for documents that will be printed directly from the word processing program onto desktop printers. Don't ever take your word processing document to a service bureau (*see Chapter 16*) for professional, high-end output. If they don't flatly refuse to do the job, they may charge you extra for recreating the job using a professional page layout program.

Word processors are also not very good at professionally formatting text—they just don't have the sophisticated features for adjusting the spacing and position of text characters, controlling hyphenation, or wrapping text around an image. If you want truly fine and beautiful type, insert your word-processed text into a page layout application such as Adobe InDesign or QuarkXPress.

The software vendors try to delude you into thinking you can create entire newsletters and brochures in word processors. Technically, you can, sort of, but it's so much trouble and there are so many limitations that believe me, you'll have much more fun creating your newsletter in a page layout application. The internal structure of a word processing page just doesn't allow you the freedom you need to make something like a newsletter, fancy brochure, advertisement, or other designed piece.

Most people start off typing their text in a word processing program and then importing or placing it into a page layout application. If you are preparing text in a word processor that you or someone else is going to insert into a page layout application, here are some guidelines to follow. (If you receive text that is typed by others, you should make a copy of this list and give it to that person.)

▶ If you use tabs to separate colums of information, **insert only one tab character between each column.** Even if the text doesn't line up correctly, don't add any extras tabs. Those extra tabs are going to cause huge gaps and uneven columns in the page layout application. If you find it difficult to read the columns, use the tab stops to even out your columns.

▶ **Use only one space after periods.** The old rule of two spaces after a period applies only to typewriters.

▶ **Don't hit the paragraph return several times to make spaces between paragraphs.** Those extra lines are only going to cause problems later on. If you need space between paragraphs, you should create it using the "Space Before" and "Space After" paragraph formatting. You can find these commands in your word processing program.

▶ Before you use tables in the word processor, find out if your layout program can import them. **However, don't apply fancy colors or borders to the table in the word processor.** That formatting will have to be removed in the page layout program.

▶ **Don't use the built-in drawing or graphics features of word processing programs.** They don't print as well as professional graphics and can cause all sorts of problems if you output your file using a professional process. The same thing applies to the clip art that ships with word processing programs.

▶ **Don't insert graphics or photographs from other applications into a word processing document.** Instead, make a note in the text that the graphic or photo goes into that spot. Then, the person doing the layout can add the graphic in the correct position.

▶ **Check before using automated formatting such as drop caps, numbered lists, footnotes, endnotes, and indexes.** You want to make sure that the page layout software will be able to import these features correctly. If not, the formatting will have to be removed and reapplied using other techniques.

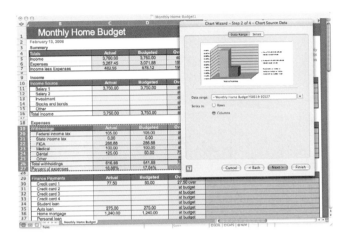

A spreadsheet and the chart options for a Microsoft Excel document

Spreadsheet applications

Spreadsheet applications, such as Microsoft Excel or Lotus 1-2-3, are used by number crunchers to do all sorts of statistical analyses, invoices, budgets, grading sheets, simple and complex forms, and more. You can use a spreadsheet to create exceptional tables to organize information into easy-to-read columns. You can convert information into charts and graphs that can be colored and formatted for presentations and printed directly from the spreadsheet application onto desktop printers. Charts and graphs from a spreadsheet can be imported into word processing documents and printed to desktop printers.

However, the information in spreadsheets does not import easily into professional page layout programs. This means you may need to convert your tables to plain text or recreate them as tables in other software to get professional-level results.

Here are some other guidelines to follow if you want to insert information from a spreadsheet into a page layout application:

▶ **Don't copy and paste charts and graphs from spreadsheet files into page layout software.** Although you may get something that looks okay on the screen, it will often cause problems when printing.

▶ **Try to use a dedicated illustration program such as Adobe Illustrator or CorelDraw to create charts and graphs** instead of a spreadsheet application. These programs have better control for colors, lines, and professional output. They are also much less likely to cause printing problems later on. One way to accomplish this is to export the data from the document as ordinary text and then import it into a program that creates tables and graphs.

▶ If you don't have access to a professional illustration program, **look for an export feature in the spreadsheet program** that allows you to export charts and graphs as PDF files. (PDF stands for "Portable Document Format" and is covered in Chapter 17.) This PDF can then be placed into the layout program.

Presentation programs

Presentation programs, such as Microsoft PowerPoint, are the electronic equivalents of the old slide shows I used to work on. Back then we filled two slide carousels and alternated between the two slide projectors. Today, with software such as a presentation program, I can create stunning slide shows with incredible extras that I can get only from computer software.

You can import graphics, as well as do some basic drawing. You can put special backgrounds on each page that blend from one color to another, add interesting textures, and create other effects that add to the impression of the presentation. You can add sounds and movies and create limited animations, like text and graphics moving in and out.

Each page of a presentation program becomes an electronic presentation slide. The computer is then hooked up to a projector that displays the presentation. You use the computer to move between the pages in the presentation.

Converting presentations for print

One of the most common questions I get from designers is how to convert their company's PowerPoint files into illustrations that can be used in annual reports, ads, and other printed documents.

Unfortunately, the files in presentation programs should not be used for professional output as part of printed designs. The backgrounds and textures are not in the proper format for color separations (*see Chapters 9 and 10 for lots of information about separating colors*), nor are the graphics.

PowerPoint files *can* be directly printed onto office printers. However, if you want those PowerPoint files to be reproduced on a commercial, high-quality press, there are two different techniques. The first way is easy; the second way is best.

The *easiest* way to professionally output from PowerPoint is to convert the presentation into a PDF file (covered in Chapter 17). This doesn't control all the colors and elements in the file, but it will create a file that can be printed at a print shop.

The *best* way to recreate your presentation takes a little more work, but the results are worth it.

1. Export all the text from the presentation into a plain text file.

2. Convert a presentation page that doesn't have any text on it into a picture format, or reproduce the backgrounds in an image editing program.

3. Insert the background image into the page layout program.

4. Insert the presentation text into the page layout program, creating one page per "slide."

5. Take this new file to the print shop for output.

Image editing programs

After you scan an image into a computer or take a photo with a digital camera, most likely you will want to make some changes to the image. You may need to clean up some dust and scratches; change the brightness, contrast, or colors; or take out the background and add other images. Whatever you plan to do, you need an image editing or photo retouching program. The most popular image editing program is Adobe Photoshop. However, there are others, such as Photoshop Elements, MetaCreations Painter, Corel Photo-Paint, and Jasc Paint Shop Pro that have similar features.

This kind of application creates images using pixels, the tiny dots on the screen, so the images are bitmapped graphics (information is "mapped" to each pixel on the screen with "bits" of electronic messages). The combination of all those pixels can hold thousands or sometimes millions of colors, and you can edit files in an image editing program pixel by pixel. You can use paintbrushes, erasers, spraypaint, and other similar tools to create or edit graphics.

Image editing programs have hundreds of features, far too many to list here—but what is just as important is what they don't do. The following are a few things you shouldn't do in an image editing program.

> ▶ **Don't include unnecessary, large areas of solid white.** For instance, if images have a lot of white space between them, it may be better to separate the images into separate files rather than make them one large graphic.

The two stacks of coins on the left started out as one Photoshop document. However, if I need to separate them into two different images, they will print faster, and take up less space, if they are split into separate files.

> ▶ **Don't increase the size of your finished artwork.** For instance, don't place the graphic in your page layout program and then enlarge it. And don't try to drag an image from one document into another and then resize it up. Because of the way a graphic is created in these programs, increasing its

physical size could make it blurry or chunky. (*For more information on this, see Chapter 6.*)

An example of what can happen when you scale an image up in size. The image on the left was scaled up to become the two larger images. In one case the scaling made the image blurry; in the other the image looks jagged.

▶ **Don't set text and effects in a page layout program if you need the text to appear as if it is part of the image.** For instance, if you want to set text to spell out a custom license plate on a photograph or a sign on a building, you do want to set the text in the image editing program. If you set it in the layout program, the text will seem to float above the image.

The text on the left is an example of text that you want to blend into the image. The text on the right was set in the page layout program and doesn't feel like it's part of the image.

▶ **Don't use an image editing program to set large amounts of text.** A program such as Adobe Photoshop even lets you check the spelling in text. But image editing programs don't have nearly the same features for formatting, searching, and working with text that a page layout program has (*see the* *chart at the end of this chapter*). You're much better off setting text in the page layout program.

▶ **Don't set text with effects in an image editing program if you can apply the same effect in a page layout program.** As a general rule (and this is a very general rule and can be easily broken, if you need to), you should try to apply text and special effects at the last stage of your layout process. For most people, this is their page layout software.

Vector drawing programs

Vector drawing programs are the most versatile and the most challenging programs to use. Some of the most popular vector applications are Adobe Illustrator, CorelDraw, and Deneba Canvas.

Image editing programs work with pixels; vector drawing programs work in mathematical boundaries called vectors. Instead of a bitmapped image made of thousands of individual pixels, the separate parts of a vector graphic are each individual objects.

An advantage of working with vectors is that you can make changes constantly to entire objects without having to make the changes pixel by pixel. For instance, if you draw a box in a vector program, you can continue to change, as often as you like, the pattern or the color inside the box, as well as the pattern, color, and thickness of its border, and you can do it with the click of a button. You can do this because each part of the box, the inside and the border, are separate *objects* that you can manipulate endlessly with the drawing tools.

In a bitmapped graphic (like those created in an image editing application), you would have to select all the individual pixels inside the box or in the border before you could change it, and the sorts of changes you could do are limited. In fact, if you wanted to change the thickness of the border, you would have to redraw it.

Unlike pixel images, which should not be enlarged, there are no restrictions on enlarging or reducing vector images because you're not resizing *pixels*—you are just changing the mathematical formula that defines the *object.* This makes drawing programs ideal for creating artwork such as logos that need to be used at different sizes.

Some vector-drawing drawing programs also have "page layout" features. This means you can create artwork in the drawing program and also import text and other graphics to lay out pages, package designs, or posters. You can then print the page directly from the vector program.

But you should never use a vector drawing program to create long document projects such as books and magazines — not even with a multi-page program such as Illustrator. Nor would you try to edit something like a photograph in a vector drawing program because a photograph cannot be separated into individual objects.

Just as some drawing programs can do page layout, page layout programs have vector drawing tools that let you create vector effects directly in the page layout program. But don't bother to use the limited shapes in a page layout program for highly complex graphics or illustrations.

What makes the more sophisticated vector drawing programs so challenging is that it can be frustrating at first to learn how to manipulate the control points (*discussed in Chapter 7*) that create the boundaries of objects. However, taking time to learn them can help you create many important types of graphics.

Here are the sort of projects that lend themselves to vector artwork.

▶ **Special type effects** You can bend, warp, distort, and otherwise apply special effects to text. You can also set type to move along a path.

▶ **Charts and graphs** Most vector applications let you take the raw data from spreadsheet programs and convert it into compelling charts and graphs. Look at the financial pages of your local newspaper and you'll see examples of vector charts.

▶ **Logos** One of the most important uses for vector applications is to create crisp logos for all sorts of companies. The primary reason for this is that the logo can be scaled up or down to whatever size is needed.

▶ **Precision and symmetrical illustrations** The mathematics behind vector illustrations makes it a logical choice for creating perfectly symmetrical art. The objects in a vector drawing can be easily rotated and duplicated in precise amounts. This is not as easily done with pixel-based software.

▶ **Technical illustrations** Along the same lines as precision illustrations, vector applications are the best choice for any sort of technical illustrations such as assembly instructions, blueprints, and schematics. Many of these illustrations are handled by computer-aided-design (CAD) software which are much more complicated than design and illustration programs such as Adobe Illustrator.

▶ **Maps** Cartographers (map makers) need the precision to create their maps as close to reality as possible. In addition to working with vector artwork, they often download raw data from satellites that is converted into vectors.

▶ **Repeating patterns** The fashion industry uses vector artwork to quickly mock up the look of next year's hot styles. Although there are specialized programs that convert the artwork into woven fabric, many designs originate in programs like Adobe Illustrator.

Some of the types of artwork that you should create in a vector illustration program. From left to right: logo, precision drawing, signage and iconography, maps and cartography, fashion repeating patterns, 3D effect.

This doesn't mean that you can't achieve similar results in a page layout program. It's just that you could find yourself working too hard in one program, when another would be much easier. Remember, you don't want to get stuck looking for oranges in a hardware store.

Page layout programs

Page layout programs are the backbone of desktop publishing. The two most popular programs are Adobe InDesign and QuarkX-Press. However, there *are* others—some, like Adobe FrameMaker, are used mostly for technical documents. Others, like Microsoft Publisher, are more basic and are designed for low-end jobs that will be printed onto desktop printers.

A page layout program is the assembly area where all the parts of a project are put together. You can write text directly in the program, but you can also import it from any word processor. You can style and format the text professionally, and import graphics, then resize and position them.

Bleed settings

One of the most important features that separates page layout software from word processing applications is the ability to create a **bleed area** around the page. A bleed is the area outside the trim that artwork extends into. The reason why you need to set a bleed has to do with how the pages of a document are cut to size.

Consider the triangles at the top corner of this book. When I set those triangles in my page layout software, I didn't stop exactly at the edge of the page. I extended the artwork off to a bleed margin outside my page.

This extra area of color ensures that if the page is not trimmed exactly right, there won't be any white area along the edge. Any time you lay out a color or photo right to the edge of a page, you need to set a bleed so the document looks right when it is trimmed. Most bleeds are set to one-eighth inch (.125").

This is an example of why you need to set a bleed area. Illustration A shows the artwork, with a bleed outside the trim (black rectangle). When this artwork is trimmed as shown in illustration B, the artwork extends right up to the edge of the trim. Illustration C shows what happens if the trim area is cut off center. The artwork doesn't have any white gaps next to the trim. Illustration D shows what happens if there isn't any bleed. If the trim is off center there are gaps in the color at the edge of the page.

In addition to a bleed, you may want to specify a **safety area** inside the page. This area is usually a one-eighth inch margin where important text and graphics do not appear. The safety area is set so that if the knife that cuts the page comes inside of the trim area, nothing important gets cut off.

Text features

Once you bring text into a page layout program (or write it directly on the page), you can do many of the same tasks you would in a word processor:

- ▶ Style and format text, either manually or using style sheets
- ▶ Check your spelling
- ▶ Find-and-change to replace text phrases or formatting

However, because you are working in a page layout program there are other things you can do with text:

- ▶ **Rotate** and **overlap** text for special effects
- ▶ Use **justification controls** to fine-tune the spaces between letters, words, and lines
- ▶ Lock the text to a **baseline grid** so it automatically lines up across columns and pages
- ▶ Change the **horizontal or vertical scale** sizes of the text

▶ Convert **text to paths** (sometimes called **outlines**) so that it can be used for graphic elements

Some word processing features such as grammar checking, editorial revision tracking, and automatic footnotes are not found in most page layout programs. This means that the bulk of text entry should be done in a word processor and only minor or simple text entry should be done in the page layout program. However, there are programs that act like editorial partners to page layout software. Those programs let you add sophisticated editorial corrections to page layout programs.

Editorial partners to page layout applications

If you work in a large organization, you may have a special editorial program that works with your page layout software. For instance, Adobe InDesign has an editorial program called InCopy that lets editors and writers make changes to text right within the InDesign layout. QuarkXPress has Quark Copy Desk.

These editorial programs add many word processing features to the page layout software. This allows you to use macros to automate text entry and formatting, track the changes to text, revert the text to previous entries, and view how many lines of text need to be cut in order to fit the copy on the page.

Graphic features

In the early days of page layout programs, all you could do was import images from other programs. If you wanted to make changes to the size, rotation, color, brightness, or other aspects of the graphic, you had to go back to the original image program.

Even when it became possible to resize, rotate, apply colors, and make other changes to the images on a page, many people were afraid to make those changes in the page layout document. They were afraid that doing so would cause problems when the document was printed. It might add to the print time or cause the image to turn out wrong.

So, what about today? Software such as QuarkXPress and InDesign allows you to apply all sorts of incredible transformations to images. You can change their colors, brightness, contrast, sharpness, transparency, and much more. So what's the deal? Do the old rules still apply?

No—almost every rule that was true back in the early days of desktop publishing has been changed by newer software and more powerful hardware. Unfortunately you may find a copy shop or print shop that will tell you not to use some special feature in a program. Some of them are just stuck in their old ruts and don't realize that their newer software and equipment can handle the tasks easily.

Other times they may have ancient equipment that truly can't handle the newer features in the software. In those instances, you may want to investigate working with a different print shop.

In my experience, I have broken almost every one of the old rules for laying out pages. And none of my jobs have ever been bounced back from a print shop!

Old wive's tales for images

The following are some of the effects that your grandmother might have told you you couldn't do in a page layout program. For the most part there is nothing that wrong with doing it today.

- ▶ **Resizing graphics.** There's nothing wrong with changing the size of an image ten percent bigger or smaller. That kind of change isn't noticeable in the final output.

- ▶ **Scaling graphics down.** Way back when I started, we were warned not to scale images way down in the page layout program. The printer processor couldn't handle that much information. Today's processors are much more powerful and scaling images down won't tax the final output.

- ▶ **Rotating graphics.** The thought years ago was that it would take too much time to do all that rotating as part of the print processing. Instead you were supposed to rotate the image in the image editing program to save print time. It's no longer a big deal. Rotate as much as you want.

▶ **Changing the colors of graphics.** Page layout programs allow you to colorize grayscale images. Although there are more professional ways to do this, there really isn't anything wrong with doing it. (See Chapter 10 for more details on these techniques.)

Installing and managing fonts

Every time you press a key on your keyboard to type a character, you are actually accessing other software—the fonts that are in your computer. It's not enough just to copy the fonts onto your hard disk. In order to use your fonts, they need to be installed as part of your computer operating system. (*See Chapter 15 for more information on working with fonts within the software.*)

There are several different ways to install fonts. You can use the controls that are built into your operating system or you can use font management software.

Installing fonts using the operating system

The easy way to install fonts is to use the controls that are part of your computer's operating system. On Windows XP and Vista, that is done by using the Fonts Control Panel. On Mac OS X it's done by using Font Book or manually adding fonts to the Library > Fonts folders. Using the operating system controls works best for those who don't need to open or close a lot of fonts each day. That's the way I work. I have a few fonts that I like and use all the time. I don't need to open and close others very often.

Using font management software

Many designers and print shops need to open a wide variety of fonts for each document they work on. Instead of using the operatiing system to install fonts, they use third-party font management software such as Extensis Suitcase Fusion or Bitstream Font Navigator. Font management has these advantages over working with the operating system:

▶ **Auto activation.** When you open a document that uses fonts that you don't have open, the font management software will automatically open the correct fonts—assuming you have access to them on your hard disk or network.

▶ **Sets.** Font management software lets you organize your fonts into sets that you can assign to specific jobs, clients, or other categories. Then, when you know you're going to work on a specific project, you can open the entire set of fonts with a single command.

▶ **Font diagnostics.** Perhaps it's because they hang around street corners smoking cigarettes, but font files can become corrupted. Corrupted fonts can cause problems in documents. Font management software alerts you if you're working with a corrupted font.

Summary of applications

This chart should help you quickly decide which type of program you should use for different projects.

☺ EXCELLENT CHOICE. YOU WON'T BE SORRY!	☺	☹ MODERATE CHOICE. YOU MAY NOT BE HAPPY.	☹	☹ BAD CHOICE. USE SOMETHING ELSE!		
	TEXT HANDLING	IMAGES AND PHOTOS	TABLES	CHARTS	LOGOS AND TECHNICAL DRAWINGS	SLIDES
WORD PROCESSING	☺	☹	☺	☹	☹	☹
SPREADSHEETS	☹	☹	☺	☺	☹	☹
PRESENTATION	☹	☹	☹	☹	☹	☺
IMAGE EDITING	☹	☺	☹	☹	☹	☹
VECTOR DRAWING	☹	☹	☹	☺	☺	☹
PAGE LAYOUT	☺	☹	☺	☹	☹	☹

Computer Color Modes

Just as different software applications are best for particular projects, there are different computer color modes that are best for particular images.

As you work in image editing and page layout applications, it's vital that you understand what the different color modes are, which one is the right one for a particular image or project, and why some color modes create file sizes that are much bigger than others. Understanding all this will help you avoid many problems later on.

The great thing about the basics of color technology is that it's one of the few standards on the computer, so understanding the color modes in general will help you in every program you use, as well as in printing color properly.

Bit depth

Before you can really understand all the color technology, you need to understand what **bit depth** is, also called *pixel depth* or *bit resolution*. You need to understand what it means when someone tells you it's an *8-bit image* or a *24-bit image*, or when they talk about the limitations of a *16-bit monitor*. You can get away with knowing as little as this: **the higher the bit number, the more colors.**

Bit depth and file size

Logically, the deeper the bit depth, the more bits of information the computer has to send to each pixel, and thus the larger the file size. A big graphic, say 8 x 10 inches, with a deep pixel depth, such as 24-bit color, will take up many megabytes of space on your hard disk. But a 1-bit image at 8 x 10 inches takes up far less space.

(However, as you'll see later, bit depth is only part of what makes a file take up space. **Resolution** is another important part of the story.)

Bitmap color mode

The term **bitmap** refers to several things. In Chapter 4 you learned that image editing programs create **bitmapped** images that you can edit pixel by pixel. When referring to color, though, **bitmap color mode** means the image is pure black and pure white. Period. Not even a single shade of gray.

A less ambiguous term for the bitmap color mode (because we can use "bitmapped" in other ways) is a 1-bit image, as I mentioned on the previous page. It's still "bitmapped" in the sense that you can edit the file in an image-editing program pixel by pixel —it's just that all of the pixels are either black or white. Think of art in the bitmap mode as the designs you could make on a kitchen floor with only black or white tiles.

My signature and some music scanned as 1-bit images. Both of these need only pure black and pure white to be properly displayed.

If you scan a 1-bit image, the scanner only captures black or white data. (Some scanner software calls this a newspaper mode.) I scan my bank checks, mortgage statements, and telephone bills into images that I store on a backup disk. These images are saved as 1-bit images because I don't need to see those documents in color.

Geeky Stuff To Know About Bit Depth

The computer screen is divided into tiny little dots called **pixels,** or picture elements. These pixels turn on or off (white or black), depending on the **bits of information** that are sent to them. Way back in 1985, pixels in computers weren't very smart. The monitors were called **1-bit monitors** because the pixels could only understand one bit of information at a time. With only one bit of information, a pixel could be one of two "colors"—it could be either white or black, on or off. Similarly, a 1-bit image consisted of only two colors. The artwork was either white or black, on or off.

Later, monitors and images got smarter. With a 2-bit monitor or a 2-bit image every pixel could understand two bits of information. With two bits of information sent to a pixel, that pixel could be any one of four "colors." It could have these choices: 11, 00, 10, or 01. In other words, both bits could be on; both bits could be off; one on and one off; or one off and one on. One of these colors is black, one is white, and the other two are two shades of gray.

Today's 24-bit monitors and images can display millions of colors. The exact number is found by multiplying 2 times 2 a total of 24 times. This is called 2 to the 24th power, and is written mathematically as 2^{24}. That comes to 16,777,216. With over 16 million colors at hand, that is enough to simulate the number of colors in nature that the human eye can recognize.

Threshold

When you scan an image in the bitmap color mode, any gray tones (if there are any in the image) are converted to either black or white. If there are various shades of gray, the scanner evaluates how light or dark they are: If a gray is above a certain level, it's converted to black; if a gray is below a certain level, it's converted to white.

You can set the level to decide which grays are converted to black or white; this is called the **threshold**. *Lowering* the threshold means only the *darker* grays will convert to black; *increasing* the threshold means the *lighter* grays will also convert to black.

Grayscale mode

In the computer, **grayscale** is an **8-bit mode**, which means there are 254 different shades of gray, plus solid black and solid white, for a total of 256 different tones.

The concept of grayscale can be confusing because in our daily conversation we refer to grayscale images as "black and white." Think about the old photographs sent out by Hollywood stars in the thirties and forties. We call those pictures "black-and-white" photos, but they're not actually black and white—there are all sorts of gray tones in the photographs. These photos are actually grayscale.

Go back to the black-and-white kitchen floor we talked about earlier. Instead of just black or white tiles, this time you have 256 different shades of gray tiles. Obviously this lets you create much more subtle images.

What to scan as grayscale

It's easy to see that "black-and-white" photographs should be scanned as grayscale. But you should also scan as grayscale:

▶ Any type of "black-and-white" sketchy illustration that has shades of gray in it, such as pencil or charcoal sketches or wash drawings.

▶ Color photos or drawings that you're going to reproduce in black and white, like on your laser printer or copy machine.

Do not scan as grayscale any line art images that need to have crisp edges. For instance, let's say you see a great cartoon that you want to reprint in your company's newsletter. (I won't get into the legal issues of doing that here.) What you *don't* want to do is print that cartoon as a grayscale image. Instead of the cartoon coming out nice and crisp, the edges will be slightly fuzzy and the lines will be shades of black, not pure black. This has been one of my biggest pet peeves when it comes to images in newspapers and magazines. Scanning line art images as grayscale makes it difficult to see small details in the image.

There are two ways to fix this problem. You can scan the cartoon as a 1-bit image with a high resolution (*covered later in Chapter 13*), or you can scan it as a grayscale image and then convert it to a high resolution 1-bit image.

Fortunately there have been enough people taking my classes to stop scanning cartoons incorrectly. And you, reading this book, will join that army of educated graphic designers.

The acronym **RGB** stands for **r**ed, **g**reen, and **b**lue. This RGB is the system monitors use to create color, using light. Monitors have three "guns" inside that "shoot" red, green, and blue light to every pixel on the screen. The computer blends these three light beams together in varying proportions to create the other colors you see. One hundred percent of all three colors produces white, which is why RGB is called an additive color model.

The cartoon on the left was scanned as a 1-bit image. Notice how the lines are pure black on a white background. Notice how the edges of the lines are crisp.

The same cartoon was then scanned as an 8-bit (grayscale) image. Look closely and you'll see how the top of the cash register is slightly shaded with fuzzy edges.

RGB mode

Scanners use RGB to capture color images. A scanner captures the varying levels of all the red, green, and blue data in an image. Each set of color information is called a **channel**. When the three channels of color are combined, the result is the full-color image.

Each of these RGB channels contains 256 shades of color. So there are 256 shades of red, 256 of green, and 256 of blue. Each channel is 8-bit, remember? The 3 channels put together create 24-bit color (3 channels times 8 bits).

Remember the kitchen tile floor? In an RGB analogy, it's as if there are three transparent "floors" (channels) overlapping each other. Each of the 256 colored tiles on one floor mixes with the colored tiles on the other floors. The combination of 3 different "floors," each with 256 levels of colors, allows for more than 16.7 million possible colors.

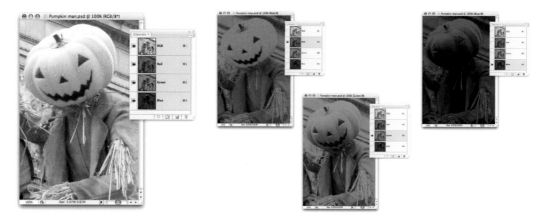

An RGB image is divided into three color channels: a red channel, a green channel, and a blue channel. Although shown here in colors, each channel is actually a grayscale image.

Choosing colors in RGB

You can never judge exactly what a color on the monitor will look like when it's printed on paper. Computer monitors use RGB; pages that are reproduced on a commercial press use CMYK colors (as discussed on the following two pages). There will always be a shift in colors from RGB to CMYK; it's physically impossible for them to appear exactly the same because they use completely different physics to display color (RGB uses light that goes straight to your eyes; CMYK uses reflected light bouncing off of a physical object). Some colors shift quite dramatically when they're converted from RGB to CMYK.

You can choose RGB colors on the screen that are bright, vivid, and neon-like. But you'll be very disappointed when your final document is printed and all the vivid, neon colors print as ordinary, dull colors. Fortunately, some programs indicate which colors can't be printed in the CMYK process. These colors are called out of gamut, which in this case means they're out of the range of CMYK (I call them "illegal" colors). In some applications, out-of-CMYK-gamut colors are indicated by a little alert symbol, as shown below. When you choose a color and see that alert symbol, it means the color you're seeing on the screen will be dramatically changed when it's converted to CMYK. Some programs let you click on the alert symbol to switch to the closest "legal" color, or you can adjust the color yourself until the alert symbol disappears.

Click the alert symbol to convert the selected color to the the closest color that is within the CMYK gamut. Even if you print to an inkjet or specialty printer that uses red, green, and blue inks, the colors won't look exactly the same as they do on the screen, for the same physical reasons—light vs. reflection. Depending on the process, however, the RGB inks from a specialty printer will usually be closer to what you expect than they will be when printed to a commercial press using CMYK inks.

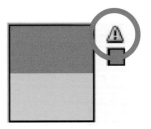

When you see the small alert symbol (circled), it indicates that the selected RGB color is out of the CMYK gamut and can't be converted to CMYK without shifting the color.

CMYK mode

The acronym CMYK stands for **c**yan, **m**agenta, **y**ellow, and a key color which is almost always blac**k**. The computer CMYK mode is used only for images that are going to be reproduced on a commercial press or on one of the specialty printers that requires CMYK, such as the Iris printer.

CMYK colors are also called **process colors**. Because the press uses these four inks to create all the colors an image needs, printing with CMYK is called **four-color printing**, or **process** printing.

The CMYK color model is based on what happens with light and objects out in the world, rather than in a monitor. A light source such as the sun or a light bulb sends white light down to objects around us; certain colors of the spectrum are absorbed by the objects and certain colors are reflected back to our eyes. For instance, when light hits a red apple, the apple absorbs (subtracts) all the colors of the light *except* the red, and the red is reflected into our eyes. In physics, this is called a **subtractive** color model.

One hundred percent of cyan, magenta, and yellow creates (in theory) black. (Remember, in RGB one hundred percent of red, green, and blue creates white.)

Similar to RGB mode (and the kitchen floor analogy), there is a channel in image editing programs for each of the four transparent colors in CMYK mode. The channels show the amounts of each process color that will be printed. These are also called the **separations** for the image. The combination of all four channels is called the **composite** image.

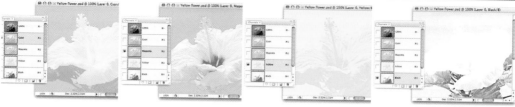

A CMYK image consists of four color channels: cyan, magenta, yellow, and black. Each channel corresponds to the ink used in process printing.

Because there are four channels, you might think a CMYK image displays more colors than an RGB image in three channels, but the four channels don't actually change the number of possible colors. In fact, there are two important things to remember when working with CMYK color on the computer:

▶ The image you see on the computer is shown to you in RGB colors, because that's what the monitor does!

▶ The actual number of colors that can be printed using CMYK inks on paper is significantly less than 16.7 million anyway.

Choosing colors in CMYK

As I explained previously, there's a difference between color on a monitor and color on a printed page. In an image such as a photograph or a scan of a painting, there's not much you can do to the individual colors to ensure they print as particular CMYK colors. But often if a job is going to be printed in full color, you also want to set a headline in color, or perhaps some rules (lines) or a background color, or maybe you want to draw a simple illustration in color. Even if you're in your page layout application, you can create colors that will print as CMYK.

But rather than choose printed colors by what you see on the screen, you should get a **process color book** or **commercial color guide** from a company such as Pantone, Tru-Match, or Agfa. These guides are available at art stores, directly from the companies and their Web sites, or often from commercial print shops.

How to use a color guide to pick a color

The best way to choose a color isn't by looking at your monitor. That color won't necessarily be the same as the final printed product. The best way to choose a color is to first look at the printed process color guide and find a color that you like.

Next, write down the name of the color (if it's from a printed color book). Or write down the CMYK values listed next to that color.

Finally, look for the name of the color in the color picker of your software program. Many programs such as InDesign, Photoshop, Illustrator, and QuarkXPress contain libraries of various commercial color guide colors. So the same color you found printed in the color picker can also be found in the software. That way you know the values are correct.

Which modes for photography and scanning?

All digital cameras take photos in the RGB color mode. When you scan a color image, you scan in the RGB color mode. Once you

---

The Index Color Mode

If you are familiar with a program such as Photoshop, you may have seen a color mode called Index Color. The index color mode is a deceptive type of color. Going back to the kitchen floor analogy, index color only has one floor, or channel, with 256 possible color tiles. But instead of limiting that channel to tints of the **same color**, the index color mode can have **many different colors** in one 8-bit channel.

Index color is rarely used in printed documents, but it is one of the most popular modes for images on the Web because you can limit the number of colors to just exactly the ones you need—fewer colors means smaller file sizes, which is always an objective in Web graphics. The most popular file format that uses the index color mode is the GIF file format.

The index mode is best used for graphics with broad areas of flat color.

---

have the photo or scanned image, you can convert it into a CMYK file before you place it into a page layout application.

It's a good idea to keep the image in the RGB mode when working in image editing programs such as Photoshop or PhotoDeluxe for these reasons:

▶ RGB images are smaller than their CMYK equivalents, so RGB images will open and save faster than CMYK images.

▶ Some effects and filters in Photoshop or other programs are only available in the RGB mode.

▶ Converting back and forth between RGB and CMYK modes will cause some loss of information in the image. Make the conversion from RGB to CMYK the very last thing you do to an image.

▶ Ask the shop that will be doing the final reproduction (commercial press, specialty printer) for any specific settings they might want you to use when converting from RGB to CMYK.

Converting from color to grayscale

Consider if you take a picture with a digital camera and then want to print that image in a black-and-white newsletter or in the newspaper. The original photo is in color, but the final printed image needs to be grayscale.

You might think that moving down from three channels of information to one is very simple, but it's actually one of the trickiest parts of image manipulation. For years designers would choose the command to convert their image without realizing that the software was making the wrong decisions.

For instance, you may want the conversion from color to grayscale to highlight certain areas of an image. If you just apply the convert to grayscale command, some colors—especially reds and blacks—can become hard to distinquish.

Fortunately the Black and White conversion dialog controls in Adobe Photoshop make it easier to control the results when converting RGB to grayscale. Instead of simply choosing the grayscale mode, the Black and White dialog box lets you adjust the settings for how the red, green, blue, cyan, magenta, yellow, and black controls are converted. The result makes a much more vibrant grayscale image.

Another problem is that some designers who print to the black-and-white office printer don't even bother to convert their color images into grayscale. This results in a very muddy conversion when the image is printed. The bottom line is that you should take the time to modify a color photo into a proper grayscale image.

Color mode and depth chart

Use the following chart as a quick recap of the different color modes. And remember, the deeper the bit depth, the greater the file size.

COLOR MODE	BIT DEPTH	# OF CHANNELS	# OF COLORS
Bitmap	1-bit	1	2
Grayscale	8-bit	1	256 shades of gray
RGB	24-bit	3	16.7 million
CMYK	32-bit	4	16.7 million
Index	8-bit	1	2 to 256 colors

Raster Images and Resolutions

Pixels and resolution are the heart and soul of working with digital photographs, art, and scanned images. It's somewhat similar to buying bed linens. At higher thread counts the sheets feel good; at lower counts they feel rough. With the proper resolution, images look good; with the wrong resolution, images look blurry or jagged.

There are two ways to determine the correct resolution. One is to memorize a set of numbers and rules and follow them by rote. That's okay until a project comes up that has slightly different requirements—then you're lost.

The other way is to understand *why* the numbers and rules were set. Then if a project comes up that's different, you'll know what to do.

This chapter covers the details of resolution for scanning and printing images. The goal is that by the end of this chapter you'll understand how to determine the correct resolution for any type of image for any project. (Of course, I'll also give you some numbers and rules to follow.)

Monitor resolution

Before we get into how to set the resolution for printing images, it's important to understand what the monitor is doing with pixels. After all, you're looking at the computer screen that holds the image for printing.

First, you need to understand the concept of **pixels**. Pixels are the "picture elements," or rectangles that create the images on a computer screen. If you hold a strong magnifying glass up to the monitor, you can actually see the rectangles and how a single color pixel fills up each rectangle.

If you look at the display preferences for your monitor, you can choose from the list of the recommended monitor resolutions. You can change the number of pixels the monitor displays. Now here's where it gets tricky. A *low* monitor resolution such as 800 pixels across and 600 pixels down gives you a total of 480,000 pixels (800 times 600). These pixels are rather *big* which is why it's hard to fit lots of windows and documents on the screen. The *lower* the resolution, the *larger* the pixels.

But if you choose a *high* monitor resolution, such as 1600 by 1200, the pixels get *smaller*. This means everything on your screen is smaller but you can fit more stuff on the screen. It also means

---

Raster (Dots) vs. Vector (Lines)

Raster refers to images, monitor displays, and computer graphics that use dots (on paper) or pixels (on the monitor). You'll also hear them referred to as bitmap images. In Chapter 4 you read that image editing programs such as Photoshop, Paint Shop Pro, or PhotoDeluxe create and work with images using the pixels on the screen, so those graphics are raster images.

You also read in Chapter 4 that vector drawing programs such as Illustrator or CorelDraw create and work with images as collections of independent lines and shapes, or objects, that are each defined by mathematical formulas. Those graphics are vector images.

As you read this chapter about resolution, this is the important difference to understand about raster and vector images: *vector images don't give a hoot about all this resolution stuff; it doesn't apply to them*. Vector images carry their resolution around in their math formulas—they will resolve to the resolution of the output device. For all the details about vector graphics, see Chapter 7.

So this chapter only applies to raster images, which is any image you have scanned, taken with a digital camera, or created in an image editing program.

that old-timers such as me can't read the type on the controls and menus. The pixels are just too damn small!

A low monitor resolution (left) displays larger pixels and larger screen items.

A high monitor resolution (right) displays smaller pixels and small screen items.

This is similar to the resolutions for high-definition flat panel televisions. An HD television screen with a resolution of 720p (pixels) has fewer pixels and less details than an HD television with a resolution of 1080p.

Image resolution

If you understand monitor resolution, you're well on your way to understanding image resolution. The same principles apply.

▶ The lower the resolution, the larger the pixels.

▶ The higher the resolution, the smaller the pixels.

Remember the kitchen floor analogy from the previous chapter? Imagine you're laying out a kitchen floor and you want to have the most beautiful, most detailed design. Which would you use: big, clunky tiles that are 1 square foot or smaller tiles that are only 1 square inch?

Obviously you'd choose the smaller tiles—the smaller the tile, the better the detail in the art. Now consider each of the tiles as the resolution of the floor. But instead of pixels per inch you have tiles per foot. Some tiles are larger at 1 tile per foot. Other tiles are smaller at 12 tiles per foot—the higher the resolution the smaller the tile.

That's the situation with pixels. Each pixel is a tile—the smaller the pixel the better the detail of your image. In the early days of computer graphics it was very easy to find artwork that had been created at the wrong resolution. Artwork—especially hand drawings—looked blocky or jagged. Designers would complain that their images had the "jaggies." Those jaggies were simply the large pixels on the edges of the art.

Common image resolution can be as low as 72 pixels per inch (**ppi**) to as high as 300 pixels per inch. Most Web graphics are created at 72 PPI. Most print graphics are created at 300 PPI. But, as with all good rules there are exceptions to these numbers.

The "cost" of pixels

So why would anyone ever worry about pixel resolution? Why not take photos with the highest resolution the camera can provide? Why not scan images at insanely high quality?

Well, consider the floor tiles. What if each tile costs a dollar (or a yen or pound or euro)? It doesn't matter how big or small the tiles are, they all cost 1 unit each.

If you're rich and don't care about the cost of the tiles, you can buy as many as you want at the floor care center. But reality says you need to worry about the cost of each pixel. And in terms of resolution, the cost of each pixel is an increase in file size.

Now, I'm not going to get into the mathematics of resolution as it pertains to file size. But suffice it to say, the only thing you need to know is **the more pixels in a raster image, the higher "cost" (file size)**.

Back when designers first started using computers, file size was a very important constraint. We constantly needed to keep the file size low to fit on the small hard drives. But today hard drive space is huge.

So is there any good reason to still worry about the size of print graphics? Large file sizes could slow down a desktop printer that processes your files if they've got more resolution than necessary. I'll cover that later in this chapter.

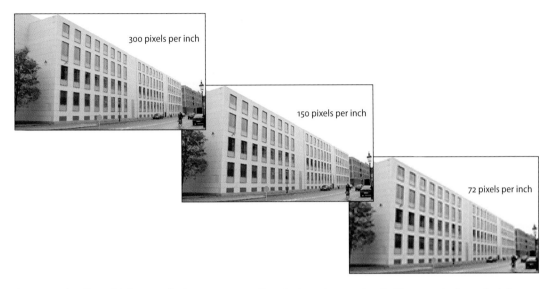

300 pixels per inch

150 pixels per inch

72 pixels per inch

An example of how higher resolution creates smaller pixels and more details. The 300 pixels per inch image has more details around the bicycle rider and the lamp post. However, the same area is just a bit of a blur in the 72 pixels per inch image.

Output resolution

Just as there's a resolution for images there's also a resolution for your printer (technically called an **output device**). The resolution for an output device is similar to image resolution: The higher the resolution, the greater the detail.

However, unlike the resolution for images, an ordinary office ink-jet or laser printer has an output resolution of anywhere from 600 dots per inch (**DPI**) to 1200 dots per inch. Obviously the higher the resolution, the better the quality. (The first laser printer I ever owned had a resolution of 300 DPI which I thought was a humongous amount!)

You may notice that image resolution is expressed as pixels per inch (PPI) whereas output resolution is expressed as dots per inch (DPI). The distinction comes from the fact that pixels are electronic elements whereas dots are little bits of printing such as laser toner or inks.

Print resolution
for grayscale or color images

All right, now that you understand what resolution is, what's the correct resolution for images that will be printed? The answer is very simple, but first you need to know the **linescreen** of the final reproduction process. Once you know the linescreen, there's a simple formula to determine the proper scanning resolution.

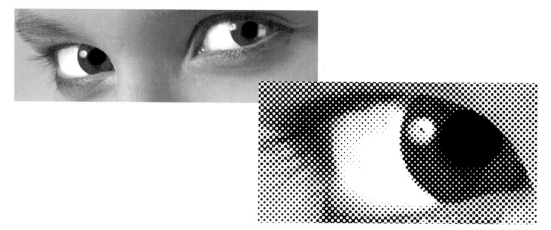

Here you can see an enlargement of the pattern of dots called a linescreen.

Understanding linescreen (lpi)

Linescreen, also known as "frequency" or "lines per inch" (**LPI**), is not computer jargon—the term has been around for many years. Printing presses print with dots of ink, so when a grayscale image like a Hollywood photo is converted for printing, the different shades of gray in the image must be converted into black or white dots. Dark gray areas are converted into large black dots, close together; light gray areas become small dots spaced farther apart; white areas have no dots.

In a full-color photograph, the cyan, magenta, yellow, and black channels of a color image are converted into dots that will be

Image Resolution vs. Output Resolution

Does it confuse you that the image resolution according to the linescreen would only be 300 PPI even though the imagesetter can output the entire file at 2540 DPI?

Well part of the reason is that the output resolution needs to be high enough so that text and line art (1-bit images) are smooth. Without a very high output resolution they would look very jagged. And remember, although you see images on your screen as a large mass of pixels, they are output as individual points of ink.

Look again at the enlarged screen in the eye on the opposite page. Although the linescreen is coarse (very large dots), each dot itself is smooth around the edges. That smoothness is only possible by the high output resolution of 2540.

printed with transparent inks that overlap each other to form all the other colors. The smaller the dots, the higher the linescreen.

Different jobs, such as magazines, books, newspapers, or brochures, are printed with different linescreens. Find the strongest magnifying glass you can, or borrow a **loupe** from a designer or a print shop (a loupe is a powerful magnifying glass used by printers to see the dot patterns in images). With the magnifying glass or loupe, look at the photos in different printed pieces.

You'll notice that the size of the dots differs between each piece. Images in newspapers are printed with big, coarse dots—you may not even need a magnifying glass to see them. Images in slick magazines are printed with much finer dots.

Linescreen specifications

As I mentioned, linescreen is measured in lines per inch, or **LPI**. In an 85-line (LPI) screen there are 85 lines of dots in one inch, both horizontally and vertically; in a 200-line screen, there are 200 lines of dots in one inch. Obviously, the higher the linescreen, the smaller the dot pattern; the smaller the dot pattern, the more detail can be printed. However, linescreen is not the same as output resolution. See the sidebar above for an explanation of this.

This book was printed with a linescreen of 150 LPI. Most magazines are printed with a linescreen of 150 LPI. High-end art books may be printed with linescreens of 200 or higher.

Linescreen and resolution

As computers and scanners became more common in printing and production, people started running tests. They looked at how an image printed after it was scanned at various resolutions. They also looked at different linescreens and what different printed resolutions looked like at different linescreens. And they came up with this general rule:

Images tend to look their best on paper when their image resolution is twice the linescreen of the finished, printed piece.

Using a resolution higher than two times the linescreen doesn't increase the quality of the printed image, but creates an unnecessarily large digital file and can slow down the time it takes to print the image. That's why I don't recommend using super-high resolutions for images.

So the following mathematical formula has become the rule to determine the correct resolution.

Image resolution equals twice the linescreen.

Simply multiply the linescreen by 2. The result is the image resolution. If you plan to print an image in a newspaper that uses a linescreen of 85 LPI, you don't need more image resolution than 170 PPI. If you plan to print an image in a magazine that uses a linescreen of 150 LPI, you don't need more than 300 PPI. Because so many print jobs are output at 150 LPI, 300 PPI has become a "standard" for resolution.

Yes, this means you *must know the linescreen of the final reproduction process before you scan or create an image.* How? Ask the right person. Or see the **Linescreen and resolution** chart on the following page.

Breaking the linescreen and resolution rules

The linescreen formula has become a guide for setting resolution; however, it's not a hard and fast rule. Many times you can get away with lower resolutions, depending on the type of image, the press, the type of paper, and many other considerations. If you want to play it safe, follow the rule.

Sometimes in the frantic pace of the production process, though, you need to resize your image in the page layout program, *which essentially changes the resolution.* Or you may need to work with images that were scanned for a different linescreen, or perhaps you need to reduce the physical size of an image (like from 4 inches to 3.5 inches).

Well, no one will send you to jail because you didn't have the perfect resolution. Your images will print. The worst that might happen if you enlarge an image is it will appear jaggy in the final printed piece, and if you reduce an image, the file can take longer than necessary to output.

Take a look back on page 85 at the three images of the building. As you can see the image at 150 PPI doesn't have all the detail of the first and the one at 75 PPI is a complete mess.

But other images are much more forgiving of the twice the linescreen rule. The clouds in the image on the next page don't look quite so bad even at 75 PPI. There just isn't much detail in the sky to lose at the lower resolution.

The clouds and sky of this image don't need a high resolution to look acceptable.

Linescreen and resolution chart

Use the following chart as a guide for the image resolution of grayscale or color images to be reproduced with different processes. This is just a guide! You really should call the print shop and ask them what they want you to use, especially if you're setting an advertisement or other project in a newspaper or magazine where there can be a wide range of linescreens.

REPRODUCTION PROCESS	LINESCREEN	RESOLUTION
Laser printer, copy machine	65 or 85	130 or 170
Newspaper	85 to 120	170 to 240
Quick-print shop, copy shop	100 to 120	200 to 240
Newsprint magazines	100 or 120	200 or 240
Glossy magazines	150	300
Offset printing	150	300
Display books	175	350
Museum-quality art book	200	400

Resolution for specialty printers

Inkjet and other non-laser printers work differently from laser printers. Because the ink is wet, it tends to spread out as it hits the paper. For this reason, the resolution of graphics for an inkjet printer can be much lower than the resolution for laser printers. The exact numbers are vague. Different inkjet printers require different resolutions. Printing onto coated paper requires a higher resolution than newsprint.

Epson, which makes a wide variety of inkjet printers, recommends a resolution of no greater than one-third the resolution of the printer. So an inkjet printer with a 720-DPI resolution doesn't need more than 240-PPI resolution. Your mileage may vary. If you don't like the results at a low resolution, use a higher one.

If you output onto a dye sub, thermal wax, or other specialty printer, check with the shop that will be making the print. Each manufacturer has their own specific formula for the proper resolution for their type of device. So read the advice in this chapter, then adjust it to fit the actual printer that will be outputting and/or reproducing your file.

Resolution for 1-bit raster images

The resolution for grayscale and color images is found by looking at the linescreen. A low (coarse) linescreen requires less resolution than a high one. But 1-bit artwork (line-art) doesn't have any screens. **Each pixel of a 1-bit image becomes one dot in the printed image on the page.**

This means that 1-bit artwork requires a higher resolution than grayscale or color artwork. For most office printers that means that the 1-bit image should be the same resolution as the output device. If the inkjet printer has a resolution of 720 DPI, then scan your line art at 720 PPI. If the laser printer has a resolution of 1200 DPI, scan your art at the same setting.

You don't need to scan a 1-bit image any higher than the output of the printer.

Imagesetter resolution for 1-bit raster images

If your project is going to be reproduced on a commercial printing press, you'll most likely have your digital files output to an imagesetter, an extremely high-resolution PostScript printer. Even though the final destination is the printing press, **the imagesetter is the final output device**.

Most imagesetters output at resolutions around 2400 DPI or 2540 DPI. So if you were paying attention in the previous section, you might expect to scan a 1-bit image at a resolution of 2400 PPI or 2540 PPI. Well, it was nice that you were paying attention, but it's not necessary or even advantageous to use such a high resolution because the imagesetter software throws away any data in the image that exceeds 1200 DPI, so 1200 PPI is the highest image resolution you need.

Changing resolution

Changing resolution is probably the most misunderstood part of working with raster images. Unlike the analogy of the kitchen floor tiles that stay one size on the floor, raster images are often scaled (resized) up or down to change the dimensions of the image (like from 3 inches to 4 inches wide). As soon as you change the dimensions of a raster image, you change its resolution. Some resolution changes are unavoidable and work out okay, but others can mean that a file that was scanned at the right resolution no longer looks so good.

Stretching pixels

Let's go back to our kitchen floor. What if we double the size of the kitchen, but we don't have more tiles to cover the space. We might have to stretch each of those tiles to twice its size. (I know it's hard to stretch tiles, but stay with me.) The pattern of the tiles enlarges to twice its size. But does the pattern have any more detail? No, the tiles are bigger, but the details stay the same. An image that looked fine at its original size doesn't look so good when stretched; it loses detail.

That's what happens when you enlarge a raster image, whether you do it in the image editing program or in the page layout application. When you originally scan or create a new file, it creates a set number of pixels. If you later increase the physical dimensions of the file (like the rubber being stretched), the pixels have to stretch and the image looks bad.

Adding pixels from thin air

But what if you could add more pixels instead of stretching them as you scale an image? In Photoshop, the term for changing the number of pixels as you change the size of an image is called **resampling**. When you resample up, the resolution stays constant as you increase the dimensions of the file.

You might see this resampling feature and say, "Aha! I have found a way to avoid the jaggies! I'll just resample the image as I increase the dimensions and thus it will keep the detail and look great." Unfortunately, resampling up doesn't work as well as getting the right resolution to begin with.

The program doesn't know what detail it's supposed to insert as it creates the new pixels. So it guesses. Unfortunately, its guesses result in a fuzzy image rather than a detailed one. If you understand what's going to happen when you increase the dimensions of an image, you can sometimes get away with it, but it's never a good idea to double or triple the physical size of a raster image.

If it's a scanned image, rescan the original art at a larger size as discussed in the next section. If it's an image from a digital cam-

Working With Proxy Images

Back in the 1990s, we used low-resolution images in our layouts and then before printing swapped them for the high-resolution file. These low-resolution files were sometimes called **proxy images** or **FPO placeholders**. The reason for this was that the hard drives on the computers were too small to hold the high-resolution graphics. Unfortunately, there are still companies stuck back in the twentieth century. They don't realize that this workflow is totally unnecessary as today's hard drives have plenty of room for the actual image. If you meet up with someone who is still working this way, ask them if they have considered upgrading to a more modern workflow.

era that can't be retaken, try the sharpening technique described later in this chapter.

Scanning and enlarging raster images

Let's say you have an old high-school yearbook photo that's only 1 inch wide. But you want to print it at 8 inches wide. How do you scan the image so that you get the correct resolution? The simple formula for scanning with "extra" resolution is this:

Divide the final width by the width of the original image and then multiply it by the desired final resolution. The result is the resolution at which you should scan the image.

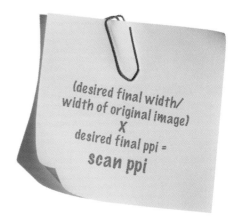

(desired final width/ width of original image)
X
desired final ppi =
scan ppi

In the case of the yearbook photo this becomes (8/1) x 300 PPI = 2400 PPI. This gives you enough pixels to resize the image to the correct resolution. (There are also controls in the scanning software that will do all the necessary math for you.)

But what if you just want to scale something ever so slightly? Like you're putting in a photograph in your brochure and you need the photo just a bit bigger. Do you really have to rescan the original?

No, says the ever-practical person. (We won't ask the purists.) For continuous-tone images like photographs, that tiny little bit of scaling won't make much of a difference at all. In fact, it's hard to see any difference in an image that is scaled less than 10 percent.

Choosing: 72 and 288 PPI? Or 75 and 300?

Some designers and photographers use 72 PPI as their low resolution standard; but others use 75. Is there a reason? Yes, and it has to do with those who don't like doing complicated arithmetic.

If you start with a 72-PPI image, you will want to increase the resolution (without resampling!) to 300 PPI. You have to multiply 72 by 4.1666… to get close to 300. So some designers use 72 PPI and then just multiply by 4 to get a high-resolution file of 288 PPI. It's much simpler.

Other designers use 75 PPI for low-resolution images and then multiply that by 4 to get 300-PPI files. Is there a big difference? Not really. 288 PPI is quite sufficient for most situations. My own preference is to use 75 PPI and 300 PPI.

Reducing raster images

Obviously there are problems with increasing the dimensions of a raster image, but what about decreasing the dimensions? It's no problem at all if you do it in the image editing program.

But if you place a raster image into a page layout program and then reduce its dimensions on the page, you do have a potential problem because even though you resize the dimensions, *the file size stays the same.* This means the computer may still send all the image data to the printer.

For instance, let's say you place a 4-inch wide photo on your newsletter page and realize you really need it 2 inches wide. The 4-inch photo is 2.3 MB; when you resize it on the page to 2 inches, there's still 2.3 MB of information in the file.

Unless you set the print controls in the page layout program to throw away any extra pixels, the computer will send 2.3 MB of data to the print processor. If you're sending the job to the office desktop printer, this could tie the machine up for a while. Fortunately, the professional print processors at large print shops can usually handle this type of excess information.

Finding and fixing missing pixels

In today's world of mega-bigga-supa-pixel cameras, it's hard to imagine you would ever not have enough resolution in an image.

But it could happen. Perhaps you forgot and set your camera to the lowest image size. Or you only had the camera in your cell phone to capture that once-in-a-lifetime moment. Is there any way to fix an image that doesn't have enough resolution? You can try **resampling up** or **sharpening** as described below.

Resampling up

A program like Adobe Photoshop or Photoshop Elements can help you enlarge an image that doesn't have enough resolution to begin with. Use the option to Resample Image and then choose the Bicubic Smoother (best for enlargements). You can then enter the settings for a new document size.

As shown below, Bicubic Smoother does avoid the jaggies associated with enlarging images, but it leaves your image a bit soft or blurry. The Nearest Neighbor option results in jagged edges. For images that require lots of details, resampling up is not a good option. But if it's just a simple photo of the family Christmas dinner, a little resampling up won't annoy Uncle Nathan.

An example of what happens when the small image is resampled up. In this case the small image of the pocket watch was scaled up 400%. In the middle image, the resampling option was set for Bicubic Smoother. This added the soft blur around the edges. In the far right image, the resampling option was set for Nearest Neighbor. This creates jagged edges in the image.

Sharpening missing pixels

You can fix the softening of an image by applying a filter such as the Unsharp Mask in Photoshop. This gives the illusion of better details by sharpening the edges between the dark and light pixels. However, sharpening can't add details that aren't there to begin with. One of the ways that I was taught to use sharpening was whenever I was about to increase the contrast on an image, I should switch to apply a small amount of sharpening instead.

An example of how the Unsharp Mask filter can enhance details in a "soft" image. Here enlarging the watch on the left has blurred some of the details. A slight sharpening on the right gives the illusion of more detail.

Can you have too much resolution?

Will a raster image look any better if you double its resolution? No —scanning at anything higher than twice the linescreen is just a waste of your hard disk space. And does take longer to save when editing the file.

However, it's a good idea if you have an ad that you're sending to a publication to make sure you send them the file at the right resolution for their linescreen. It's only polite not to take up too much space on their hard disk.

Vector Images

Vector images are very different from raster images. For one thing, vector images are created directly in the computer instead of taken by a digital camera or scanned. And instead of using millions of tiny pixels, vector art is generated using mathematics to create individual objects. This is why vector art is sometimes called "object art."

Vector art is the primary type of artwork used for all sorts of illustrations and graphics that don't contain digital photographs or scanned images. Almost all corporate logos are designed as vector graphics. Depending on the artist's style, vector illustrations can look like cartoons, woodcuts, watercolors, or pen-and-ink illustrations. There are even some artists whose vector images look like photographs.

Types of vector art

Vector graphics can be created in color, shades of gray, or black and white. Unlike bitmapped raster graphics, though, there is a much smaller difference in file size between color, grayscale, or black-and-white vector art.

Vector graphics aren't always created in a drawing program. Some spreadsheet programs create pie charts or bar graphs in vector format. There are tracing programs that automatically convert raster images into vector images. You can also go online or purchase disks that contain many different types of vector clip art.

Advantages of vector art

There are several advantages to creating and using vector images.

Resolution

One of the major advantages of vector art is that it's resolution independent. This means it prints at the resolution of the

Examples of different types of vector art styles.

output device. The result of this is that no matter how much the artwork is enlarged or reduced, it looks great—no jagged edges. This makes vector art ideal for creating logos, maps, and other smooth-edged images that will be used at different sizes depending on the types of publications they're placed into.

Easily modified

Another advantage is that, unlike raster images, vector images can be easily modified. As we mentioned earlier, vector graphics are composed of individual objects or shapes; each of the individual objects can be moved, recolored, or reshaped endlessly. It would take many hours of work to make similar changes in raster images. This means vector art can be reworked for many different situations. If you're given the choice of illustrations created in vector or raster format, the most versatile choice (if you're going to print it) is vector.

Smaller file sizes

The mathematics of vector art allow very large shapes to be described using extremely small amounts of data. This means the file sizes of vector images are much smaller than the equivalent raster images.

For instance, if you draw a 1-inch square at a resolution of 300 PPI, there are 90,000 pixels in the square. If the square is in CMYK color, there are 4 channels of 90,000 pixels each—that means a file size of around 352 K even before you actually add color. However, the same square created as vector art is defined only with X and Y math coordinates for its starting point, width, and height. The color is also defined using a set of instructions, not four channels of pixels. So the information needed to create a 1-inch vector square is only 8 K. (You may find a larger file size if you test this in your own vector-drawing program. That's because those programs include colors, symbols, and drawing tools that add to the size of the file.)

Examples of how vector artwork can be modified. The original artwork is on the left. The middle illustration shows a change in the screen color as well as changes in the details of the microphone and speaker grill. The illustration on the right shows how the color of the case can be changed.

Challenges of vector art

With everything in life, there are challenges along with advantages. The same holds true for the challenges of working with vector illustrations.

Learning curve

Working in a vector drawing program can be more difficult than working in an image editing program, especially if you want to create subtle blends, contours, and shadows. Many people find it takes a long time to learn how to combine shapes and control colors and tints.

Vector art uses **Bézier curves** (pronounced "bay-zee-ay"). Years ago, rounded forms had to be laboriously plotted with individual points. Then the French mathematician Pierre Bézier created formulas that could describe curves using math instead of individual points. In vector programs you adjust the shapes of curves by changing the length and direction of the Bézier handles, as shown on the following page.

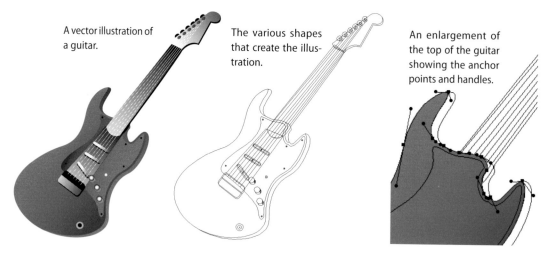

A vector illustration of a guitar.

The various shapes that create the illustration.

An enlargement of the top of the guitar showing the anchor points and handles.

Image limitations

If you're trying to create a realistic sort of image, such as a portrait, in a vector drawing program, you'll find it difficult to create contours, shadows, and highlights that look natural. To create these types of effects can require hundreds of objects in an illustration, each object colored slightly differently. It would be better to use a raster program to create a realistic portrait.

Vector Art In Product Illustrations

It takes a lot of time to create vector artwork with a photorealistic style. Yet many artists work exclusively in that style. I asked Brad Neal of Thomas Bradley , LTD, a design and illustration firm why his clients request vector illustrations.

"Originally we created our work in vector format because the clients needed the flexibility to publish it in different sizes. We've had artwork that started out on the side of a kid's toy box and then was blown up to fit the side of a tractor-trailer truck.

"Later on, companies would come to us to create artwork for products that didn't exist yet. They had the engineering specifications but the actual product hadn't been manufactured. We used their CAD (computer-aided design) drawings to create photorealistic drawings of their products. These illustrations could be used in user manuals, sales brochures, or advertising—even when the actual product was months away from finish.

"We've also worked with manufacturers, such as car companies, who want to take the previous year's product and modify it for the next year's catalog. It's easier to change the shape of a headlight in a vector illustration than it is to change the lights on an existing car."

Transparent and opaque shapes in vector art

If you work with vector graphics that you create yourself, you're probably well acquainted with each graphic and with all its various parts. But if you trace images, use vector graphics from clip art collections, or if someone gives you vector art to place into a page layout program, you may be surprised to find some areas in an image are transparent that you thought were white, and other areas are solid white that you thought were transparent.

If transparent shapes should be white

To prevent the problem shown below, in the vector program make sure the areas that look white are actually white objects. (See the following page for information about the opposite problem, white shapes that should be transparent.)

The image on the left looks fine when sitting alone on the page. But when the image is placed over other background art in the middle image, the transparent areas in the woman's face become a problem. The image on the right has been fixed by adding white patches for the woman's face and hair.

If white shapes should be transparent

To prevent the problem shown on the next page, where the spaces inside the handles are opaque, you need to create a compound path (some programs might call it a composite path). You select the outside path as well as the inside one and apply the command. The inside path then punches a transparent hole in the outside path.

On a white background, the hole in the cup on the left looks fine. However, when the cup is placed over a colored background, in the middle image, the hole in the cup stands out as a white shape. When the hole in the cup is joined to the cup in the image on the right, a transparent object is created. This is the proper way to create transparent areas in vector art.

Placing vector images in layouts

One of the most common questions I get asked about using vector images is why the preview of the image looks so bad in page layout programs. People are always concerned that the image is going to print poorly. So why do vector graphics look so bad in page layout software?

The reason has to do with something called the *preview*. The mathematical shapes that make up a vector image need to be previewed as a bitmapped graphic. The problem is that the bitmapped graphic doesn't show up as smooth vector lines. Rather it looks like very chunky graphics.

When I work in InDesign, I have several choices for how my vector artwork is displayed. Some of those choices are better than others. Ordinary Illustrator and EPS files look very jagged at the typical display setting. (Similar preview issues happen when I work in QuarkXPress.)

Fortunately these are just preview issues. The files always print with their proper display. But it does freak people out when they see those jagged previews.

Vector Art on the Web

The same mathematics that keeps file sizes small for print artwork also keeps file sizes small for vector art on the Web. One popular file format for Web files is the SWF (Shockwave Flash) format. Many Web artists use programs such as Adobe Illustrator to create SWF animations.

Although the vector image on the right looks fine when printed, its preview is terrible when viewed in a page layout program.

Vector/pixel quiz

Vector artwork is pretty easy to spot. Any artwork that is very crisp with clean edges is most likely vectors. On the other hand, the pixels in bitmapped files are soft and fuzzy. (My cat's name is Pixel and she's very soft and fuzzy.) Type always starts out as vectors, but can get converted to pixels along the way.

See if you can tell, just by looking, if the following images are vectors or pixels. Hint: Some of the images may be pixels with vector parts and others may be vectors with pixel parts.

Artwork 1

Artwork 2

Artwork 3

Artwork 4

Artwork 5

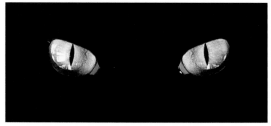

Artwork 6

Artwork 7

Artwork 8

Vector/pixel quiz answers

Artwork 1

The image of the cat is a photograph and so has to be pixels. But the red string with the gold loop are vectors added in the page layout program. Notice how they feel like they float over the photograph.

Artwork 2

The art started out as a photograph, but was then traced using the Live Trace feature in Illustrator. This converted it into vectors.

Artwork 3

The cartoon is 100% vectors. No pixels were consumed in the creation of the art.

Artwork 4

The illustration is all vectors. Even the shades of gray that might appear to be soft pixels are gradients that were created in the vector illustration program.

Artwork 5

Those two spooky eyes are definitely pixels.

Artwork 6

This one is a little tricky. Most of the cartoon is created from vectors. But there's a slight glow around the eyes. That glow comes from a pixel effect added in the illustration program. This is a good example of pixels and vectors living side by side.

Artwork 7

This is another tricky one. Almost all of the illustration is comprised of vectors. But if you look closely, you'll notice a slight blur around the edges of the blue areas. That's an effect called feathering that always creates pixels.

Artwork 8

You might not be able tell from the small version, but this art is all vectors. The artist created the cat by drawing thousands of individual objects as shown in the enlargement below.

File Formats

Every time you create a document or a graphic on the computer, the program saves that graphic with a particular file format, or internal structure. Some formats are raster, others are vector; some are high resolution, others are low resolution; some are specific to a certain type of computer or even to a certain application, others can be used by any computer or application, etc.

Just as different software programs are good at performing different tasks, different file formats are good for different purposes. For instance, some file formats are good for reproducing on office printers, but not on commercial presses; some are best for high-resolution printing; others are excellent for low-resolution Web graphics. Some file formats become the "translation device" to transfer a graphic from one program to another.

Just as you wouldn't want to spend hours working on a file in the wrong program, you wouldn't want to spend hours working on a file in the wrong format. This chapter will help you understand the different file formats and help you choose the right one for each project.

Native file formats

When you save a document in the same format as the program you're working in, that document file is in that program's **native file format**. However, native file formats are usually special formats that other applications made by competitors don't always understand. This is why you usually have to save the native file in some other format if you want to use the file in another program.

Native Photoshop files

There are far too many choices for native graphic files to cover them all here. However, given how many people use Adobe Photoshop, I will start with working with native Photoshop files (PSD).

The native Photoshop file format usually has some advantages over other formats when you're working in the native application. For instance, the native file format for Photoshop allows you to work with layers so one part of an image can be easily moved around. These layers are lost when you save the files as a JPEG or EPS file.

Major layout programs such as Adobe InDesign or Quark XPress allow you to import native Photoshop files as well as turn the visibility of the layers on or off.

However, not all page layout programs do import native Photoshop files. For instance, Microsoft Publisher requires TIFF or JPEG or some other file format. Apple's Pages application does recognize native Photoshop files, although it doesn't give you the option to control the layers within a Photoshop file.

The bottom line is that you should find out if your page layout software accepts native files from Photoshop. If it does, use the native file formats whenever possible. If not, you may have to save the file in two formats: the native PSD file as well as another file for import into your page layout program.

Photoshop file options

FEATURE	INCLUDED	NOTES
Layers	Yes	
Alpha channels	Yes	
Transparency	Yes	
Spot colors	Yes	
Annotations	Yes	
Vector paths	Yes	
PostScript text	Yes	
Vector shape layers	Yes	

Native vector files

Most applications don't accept the native file format for Corel-Draw or other vector illustration programs—with one notable exception. The native file format for Adobe Illustrator files (.ai) can be placed in many layout programs, including the high-end InDesign and QuarkXPress as well as the more pedestrian Microsoft Publisher and Apple Pages. What's that all about?

Well, the answer is less about the popularity of Illustrator and more the addition of something called a "PDF preview" in the native Illustrator file. This PDF preview makes the native Illustrator file look like a PDF file to page layout programs. And most programs allow you to place PDF files as images.

Non-native file formats

The type of file formats that each software program can create or accept, besides their own native formats, is an ever-changing situation. A company may add a new file format to its "Open File" or "Save As" capabilities to add new features or to keep up with the newest technology. For instance, Adobe Illustrator can open the files created by the old Macromedia FreeHand program. Watch out, if you convert one file format to another. Some features may get lost in translation.

Exporting or saving as non-native file formats

You can create a variety of non-native file formats in almost any software program. Depending on what you need to do, you might Export a file, or Save As with a different name and format, or you might find a menu command called something like "Send To." In Photoshop you can *save* in a number of different file formats (shown below), and you can also *export* as others. There are slight differences between exporting and saving, but both techniques create non-native file formats. Check your manual for details.

Importing and opening non-native file formats

When you bring a non-native file into an existing page of a page layout application, it's called **importing**. Most programs have an **Import** command, or it might be called **Insert**, **Get Picture**, or **Place**. Check your manual. Typically importing adds the file, such as a computer graphic or a scanned image, to an existing page.

Instead of importing, some applications just open non-native files like they would their own native format. For instance, Adobe Illustrator can open FreeHand files and many raster images from any other drawing application. If you go to the Open File menu and see a file listed in the box, that usually means the application can open and display it.

TIFF files

The TIFF format **(Tagged Image File Format)** is a raster (bit-mapped) file format. Almost every raster program, such as an image editing or paint program, can save TIFF files, and almost every other application can place or import TIFF images. These files are extremely flexible—a TIFF can be CMYK, RGB, grayscale, index, or bitmap format, any bit depth, and any resolution. TIFF is also a good format for files that need to move between Windows and Macintosh computers.

TIFF compression

Compression means the information in a file is squished so the file takes up less disk space. When you save a TIFF file, you are given the option to apply LZW or ZIP compressions. These compressions are called **lossless**. Lossless compression means no data is lost (lost-less) when the file is compressed, so the image looks exactly the same when it's compressed as it does when it's not compressed. You are also given the option to apply JPEG compression which is **lossy** (see page 118).

TIFF file options

FEATURE	INCLUDED	NOTES
Layers	Yes	
Alpha channels	Yes	
Transparency	Yes	Not all programs can read the transparency in TIFF files
Spot colors	No	
Annotations	No	
Vector paths	Yes	
PostScript text	No	
Compression (lossless)	Yes	
Compression (lossy)	Yes	

EPS files (pixel)

EPS stands for Encapsulated PostScript. With an EPS file, all the pixel information in the image is packaged together with added information that is not usually contained in an image file.

Years ago, the only way to save information such as the vector paths that would clip or silhouette a file was in an EPS file. However, these days, that information can be saved in a TIFF file.

You may hear some people insist that they must save their pixel files in the EPS format. They don't really have to unless they are working with some very specialized printing equipment. Native Photoshop or PDF files can do everything an EPS file does—and more!

EPS file options

FEATURE	INCLUDED	NOTES
Layers	No	
Alpha shannels	No	
Transparency	No	
Spot colors	No	
Annotations	No	
Vector paths	Yes	Vector paths will be rasterized if the EPS is reopened.
PostScript text	Yes	Text will be rasterized if the EPS is reopened.

EPS files (vector)

Vector programs such as Adobe Illustrator and CorelDraw let you save files in the EPS format (Encapsulated PostScript). As I discussed at length in Chapter 7, the graphics in a vector EPS file are composed of a number of separate objects, each one defined mathematically. A vector EPS file will print at whatever the resolution is of the printer, and it can be enlarged and reduced with no degradation of the image at all.

DCS files

The DCS format (Desktop Color Separation) is a variation of the EPS file format. The DCS format was developed by Quark Inc. to allow QuarkXPress to read and print CMYK files correctly. These files can be printed only to PostScript printers.

Years ago service bureaus would require DCS files in order to create color separations. Fortunately those days are past and it is very rare to find a service bureau that asks for DCS files.

PICT files (Macintosh)

The PICT file format (PICT is short for "picture") was created long ago by Apple for images on the first Macintosh systems. A PICT file can contain both vector and raster information. A pixel-based program such as Photoshop exports PICT files only in pixel (raster) format; a vector program exports its PICT files in vector format.

The PICT file format is stupid. It uses a very primitive language to encode its data. To compare languages: PICT is pig latin; PostScript is Shakespeare. Because of this, PICT files cause printing problems, especially on PostScript printers and high-resolution imagesetters. If you can, avoid saving as a PICT file.

BMP files (Windows)

Windows has a BMP format (Windows Bitmap) that's just about as stupid as the PICT format on the Mac and will cause similar printing problems. If you can, avoid working with BMP files.

WMF files (Windows)

The WMF file format (Windows Metafile) is a vector format for use on the Windows platform. Like PICT or BMP files, it can create printing problems.

GIF files

The GIF file format (Graphical Interchange Format, pronounced "gif," not "jif," because it stands for "graphical") is a compressed graphic format that can be displayed on any computer. It was originally created by the CompuServe online service for transferring images through the phone lines. Because of these features—small files that can be viewed on any computer—GIF images are found everywhere on the World Wide Web.

There is no use for the GIF format in professional printing. If you download a GIF image from the Web, you can certainly print it on an office printer without any problem, but it probably won't look very good because most Web graphics have a low resolution of 72 pixels per inch. A GIF file doesn't *have* to be 72 PPI, but because a higher resolution doesn't look any different on the screen, Web graphics are always (or should always be) 72 PPI.

If you need to use the same image for both the Web and in printed documents, make two copies of the file: one as a printable TIFF and the other as a Web GIF.

PNG files

The PNG file format (Portable Network Graphic, pronounced "ping") is similar to GIF in that it is designed as a compressed format. It was created to provide a royalty-free format to CompuServe GIF files. PNG files can support 24-bit color (millions of colors) and transparency without the jaggy edges so prevalent in GIF images.

In theory PNG files can be used for either Web graphics or in printing. But most people don't use PNG files at all.

However, **PNG files are terrific for use with the Microsoft Office applications**. If you need to get a vector logo into a PowerPoint presentation, save it as a PNG file with transparency. PNG files print perfectly from any of the Office applications.

JPEG files

If you have a digital camera, most likely you're already working with JPEG files. The JPEG file format (Joint Photographic Experts Group, pronounced "jay peg") is one of the most popular formats for digital cameras because it allows you to compress the image into a much smaller file. This means you can store more images on the camera. The JPEG format is used for photographic images instead of the GIF format because in a JPEG you have the full range of 24-bit color.

JPEG compression

The JPEG format is a *lossy* compression. When you save a file as a JPEG, a certain amount of data is thrown away and you can't get it back. You can compress JPEG files quite a bit before you notice

Resaving a JPEG File

The little bit of compression that is applied to stock photos or files taken with a digital camera isn't really a problem. I have a good friend who is a professional news photographer and he saves his work as JPEG files with a slight compression. Those photos print in major magazines without any problems. However, once you open a JPEG file and start working on it, you really shouldn't resave the file as a JPEG image. You're applying more compression to an image that has already been compressed. That double compression is more noticeable than what the file had originally.

For instance, some of the images in this book are JPEG files downloaded from photospin.com. Some of these I placed directly into the layout without converting. They look fine.

I took other images and worked on them in Photoshop. I didn't resave them as JPEG files as that would have been applying two sets of compression. So I saved those files in the native Photoshop format which doesn't apply compression.

it, but you will eventually see the degradation on the screen and especially in the print output.

An example of what JPEG compression does to an image. The image on the left has the maximum quality and lowest compression applied. The image on the right has the minimum quality and highest compression.

You can choose how much compression to apply to the image:

more compression = smaller file size, but lower quality

less compression = larger file size, but better quality

Your decision about how much compression to apply is directly related to your use of the image. Sometimes you need a smaller file size, for example, to send over the Internet, and so you have to accept slightly lower quality. Other times you might need the quality, like in a computer presentation, more than you need the smaller file size.

Some professional stock photo companies save their images with JPEG compression. It may be the very least amount of compression, but it does mean that some detail has been lost. And although most people can't tell the difference, it doesn't seem right to throw away detail just to cram a few more images onto a CD. If you do get JPEG stock photos, open the files in your image editing program and save them as either native Photoshop or TIFF files. (*See Chapter 14 for more details about using stock photos.*)

PDF files

The PDF file format (Portable Document Format) is a file format that embeds, right within the file, all the necessary information to view a single document or an entire publication: text, images, page breaks, fonts, etc.

Many software manuals are now included as PDF files on the software CD; when you double-click the PDF, it opens in the free Adobe Reader software. This way you see the document exactly as it was originally created.

The PDF format is also the format that many print shops ask people to use when sending finished documents. Because PDF is so important, I'll cover it in detail in Chapter 17.

PostScript files

PostScript is a "page description language" from Adobe Systems that tells an electronic printer exactly how to "image" the data from the computer onto a piece of paper. Many years ago, print shops would ask designers to create PostScript files. However, these days most print shops request PDF files.

If your print shop requests a PostScript file, ask them if they will accept a PDF, which is much easier to create.

If you need to create a PostScript file for a high-resolution printer, make sure you get specific instructions from the service bureau. They may need to give you special software, called a *printer driver*, so you can set all the options correctly for their particular imagesetter. A PostScript file made for a desktop laser printer won't always print properly on a high-resolution imagesetter.

Which format to choose?

As a general rule, if you can, keep a file in its native file format as long as possible. If you can print directly from Photoshop or Illustrator, do so. If you need to place a file into a page layout program, see if the program will accept the native files from Photoshop or Illustrator.

If you can't use the native file format, your next best choice is to export or create a PDF file. In the unlikely event that you can't use a PDF file, then choose TIFF for images and EPS for vector files.

Format quiz

The following quiz lists different types of projects that you might work on. Choose the correct format for each project. There may be more than one correct answer for each project. Answers follow the quiz.

Project #1

You are working on images taken from a digital camera. What format might the images come in from the camera?

A. JPEG B. TIFF C. PSD D. PDF

Project #2

You make adjustments to the photographs in project #1. You are going to use the images for a printed brochure. What format(s) should you *not* save the images as?

A. GIF B. TIFF C. PSD D. JPEG

Project #3

You are going to use the photographs from project #1 on a Web page. Which format(s) might you use for the Web?

A. GIF B. JPEG C. PNG D. PSD

Project #4

You've hired a designer to create a logo for your company. Which application should she use for the final graphic?

A. Photoshop B. A vector-drawing program C. A Web layout program D. Microsoft Word

Project #5

Your print shop has asked you to create a PDF of your page layout. What will you need to send along with the PDF file?

A. Fonts only B. Image only C. Fonts and images D. Nothing

Project #6

You have a press release that you want to send to many magazines. What's the best format to ensure the editors will read the release exactly as you've written it?

A. PDF B. GIF C. Photoshop D. Microsoft Word

Project #7

You want to set the images in your digital camera to be the highest quality. How should you set the camera options?

A. JPEG with high compression B. JPEG with low compression C. TIFF with no compression D. PDF file

Format quiz answers

Project #1

Most likely A, JPEG files although there are some digital cameras that will save in the TIFF format (B).

Project #2

Answers A and B. GIF should be used only for Web pages. JPEG should not be used if the image was originally saved with compression. TIFF and PSD are fine to use in a print project.

Project #3

Answers A, B, or C. All three are acceptable Web formats. PSD is not used for Web graphics.

Project #4

Answer B. A vector-drawing program is the best format.

Project #5

Answer D. Nothing. That's one of the benefits of the PDF format. Everything can be contained in the file.

Project #6

Answer A. PDF.

Project #7

Answer C gives you the highest quality. But if your camera doesn't save as TIFF, then answer B. I don't know of any digital camera that saves in the PDF format.

THE WORLD OF COLOR

Do you dream in color? Many people report dreaming only in black and white. But some scientists say all dreams start out in color, Then the color fades along with the details of the dream. No matter what your dreams, here's how to add color to your printed pages.

Process Color Printing

If you read Chapter 5, you know all about the different modes of color on the computer. But this book is about getting pages printed, so you also need to know about how color is printed on the page. Printing presses use two basic methods.

One method is called "process color," which creates the full-color images you are accustomed to seeing in magazines, posters, CD covers, etc. This method uses four separate, transparent inks that overlap each other to create all the colors you see. It's expensive; four-color process is usually only attempted by large presses.

The other method is "spot color," which uses one color of ink from a tube of ink for each area you want colored on your page. I cover spot color in Chapter 10.

What are process colors?

Process is a description applied to the four transparent ink colors that are combined to make full-color images. The four **process colors** are **cyan** (a blue color), **magenta** (the closest process ink to red), **yellow**, and **black**.

Remember, printing presses print dots. To make full-color images, the press combines yellow dots and cyan dots to make green; magenta and yellow dots to create red; cyan and magenta to create royal blue; and so on. You should recognize this from Chapter 5 as the **CMYK color mode**.

Process color chart

The following chart shows how process colors are created.

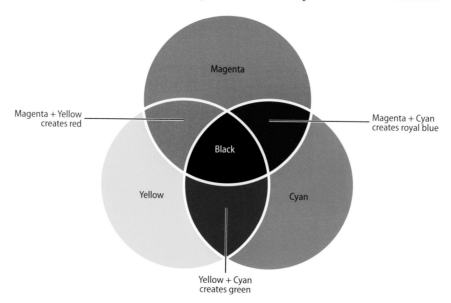

You'll notice the chart only uses three inks to make black. So why isn't process printing just CMY (cyan, magenta, and yellow) rather than CMYK? Well, the three colors create black only in theory; in practice, the three colors create a very muddy, dark brown. So black is added to get a nice, rich black color. Black is also used to give more depth to the other colors.

Defining process colors

Process colors are "defined," or created, by specifying exactly how much of each of the four colors should be used in combination. "How much" is defined in percentages. For instance, solid black is 100 percent black and 0 (zero) percent of cyan, magenta, or yellow. These four percentages are always written in the same order of the abbreviation CMYK. So a simple black would be written as 0:0:0:100. Sometimes the colors are written with the letters C, M, Y, and K in front of the percentages. So simple black would be written as C: 0, M: 0, Y: 0 K: 100. You can create thousands of different colors using combinations of the four process colors.

The different desktop publishing programs create process colors all in the same way: You define a color with percentages of the CMYK inks. So if you want an orange color to work with, you find the color palette in that program and enter something like 60 percent magenta and 80 percent yellow (and no cyan or black). If you want a darker orange, add 20 percent black. Once you define a color, you can apply it to text, art, backgrounds, etc.

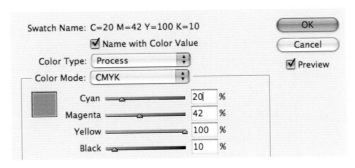

An example of how process colors are defined in a page layout program such as InDesign.

CMYK colors only in a CMYK job!

Your software will also let you define colors using different color modes, such as RGB. Don't do that if you're going to print with process colors! Remember the illegal colors we talked about in Chapter 5, the RGB colors that cannot be printed using process inks? Not only will the color come out differently from what you expect, but you can mess up your files so they won't print properly. Commercial printers hate it when designers put RGB art and colors in the file that will go to press. Make clean files: Use only CMYK colors for process color printing.

What are separations?

Separations are an important part of process colors. Because all of the colors are made from four transparent inks, the printing press only needs four **plates** to print from. A printing plate is not like a dinner plate — it's a piece of photographic film, or sometimes paper (or sometimes rubber or metal). If you want to understand plates, try the experiment on page 130.

Remember all that stuff in Chapter 5 about linescreens and halftones and dots? Well, when you output a CMYK file to your printer, the printer uses the linescreen value to **separate** the four colors into four sets of **dots**; each CMYK plate contains the range of dots that create the various color values.

Consider the illustration of the American flag shown on the opposite page. The red is a combination of 100 percent magenta and 100 percent yellow (C:0, M: 100, Y: 100, K: 0). The dark blue in the flag is a combination of 100 percent magenta and 100 percent cyan (C: 100, M: 100, Y: 0, K: 0). And let's put a black outline around the flag (C: 0, M: 0, K: 100). Between the three colors, red, dark blue, and black, we need dot combinations of four inks: cyan, magenta, yellow, and black. (The white stars and stripes will be the white of the paper.)

To print the image of the flag, these colors need to be separated onto their own plates. This means the area that creates the dark blue of the flag (called the canton) appears on two pieces of paper or film: one for the magenta plate and one for the cyan plate. The red in the canton and stripes is separated onto two pieces of paper or film: one for the magenta plate and one for the yellow

---

Why Does K Stand For Black?
So why is the letter K used for the Black plate? When I first started in print production I was told that originally the Cyan plate was called the Blue plate. And so the letter B was already used. So they chose the K in Black. As nice as that story sounds, it's not true.
The actual reason is that the Black plate is also called the **key color** or key plate. When photographs are printed, it is the Black plate that contains all the detail in the image. This is where the K comes from. So the next time someone asks, you'll know the answer.

plate. Now, because the canton and stripes both use magenta to make their colors, the magenta plate will contain both the canton and the stripes as shown in the illustration below. The cyan plate only contains color where the canton is. And the yellow plate only displays the stripes. The black will have its own plate of an outline around everything. Thus the four plates of cyan, magenta, yellow, and black are called the **separations**.

The cyan, magenta, yellow, and black plates for the four-color flag illustration.

Channels and plates

If these four plates seem the same as the four channels in a CMYK image, it's because they are: The channels of a CMYK image print onto CMYK plates. When all four colors are combined on the paper, the result is a full-color image. In fact, it was this ability to electronically separate colors that made desktop publishing software so important to designers and artists. It used to take several days to separate the four colors using a photographic process for each image and piece of type, then "stripping" it all together onto the plates; now it can be done in a matter of hours.

What color are separations?

You might think that the information on the cyan plate is cyan and the magenta plate is magenta. But when documents are separated, they are actually output as black and white onto either paper or film. The color comes from the ink on the press; the cyan plate will be used to print the cyan ink, etc.

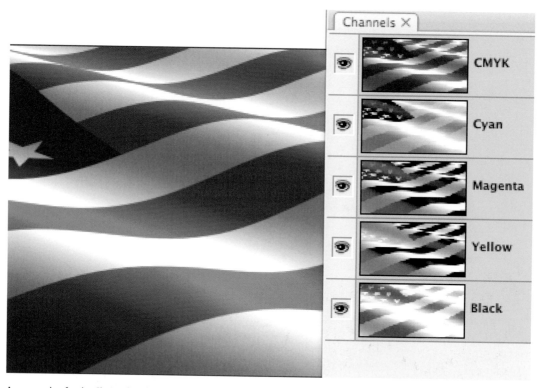

An example of a the Channels palette for a four-color image. Notice how each of the channels corresponds to the four colors in process printing.

See for yourself!

Try this experiment: Open a CMYK image. In your software printing dialog box, choose the option that says "Separations" and click Print. You will get four pages, each in black toner. Each page is a separation. Each one of these separations is essentially a plate, very similar to what the print shop will put on the press, except their plates are higher quality than your desktop printer.

If you try this and you get five or six or seven plates, it means there are extra colors in your file that are not CMYK. Now there are times you print with extra colors (*see Chapter 10*), but generally you want to make sure your file will only output the four CMYK plates. Don't let the print shop discover that for you.

Color dot screens

When you specify a color as 100 percent, that color is represented as a solid black area in the separation. When you specify anything less than 100 percent, the color is screened as a dot pattern. For instance, a 10 percent black consists of a series of small dots in a pattern. A 50 percent black has the same number of dots, but they are larger, which creates a darker area. A 90 percent black has even larger dots, creating an even darker area. The number of dots is determined by the linescreen, as I discussed in Chapter 6. Once the linescreen is established, the number of dots doesn't change—the size of the dots changes.

Three dot patterns for 10% black (top), 50% black (middle), and 90% black (bottom). As the dots become larger, the color becomes darker.

Moiré patterns

If you have a color such as orange that consists of 50 percent magenta and 50 percent yellow, the color is created by overlapping two dot screens: magenta and yellow. Exactly how these two screens overlap is *critical*. The goal is for your eye to see only a blend of the two colors, not the two sets of individual color dots. However, if the screens don't overlap correctly, you see an optical effect called a **moiré pattern** (pronounced "mwah-ray") instead of the blended color.

Avoiding moiré patterns

There are several ways to accidentally create moiré patterns. One is to scan an image that was already printed on paper, which means it was printed with a dot screen. The combination of the original screen in the printed image with the dot screen of the image when it is printed again may cause a moiré pattern.

Another way to create a moiré pattern is to use the wrong **screen angles**. Fortunately, you won't have to set those screen angles yourself. That's something the print provider should handle. However, you should understand what screen angles are doing.

Trivia

Moiré patterns don't happen just in printing. Television screens show a moiré pattern when a striped shirt is displayed at certain angles. The image seems to vibrate when the shirt is shown. You can also see a variety of moiré patterns by taking two window screens and overlapping them together. As you rotate one screen next to the other, you'll see the moiré pattern appear and disappear.

Choosing screen angles

Long before computers, print shops needed to avoid moiré patterns. They discovered that if the separate color dot screens were tilted at different angles, it helped avoid moirés. They discovered specifically that a 30-degree difference between screen angles made it even less likely that moiré patterns would develop. So they assigned different angles to each of the colors.

The black plate was assigned a 45-degree angle. This is because a 45-degree angle is the least noticeable to our eyes; it makes the strong, black color less obvious when combined with other colors. And black is often printed alone, as in a grayscale photograph; if the line of dots were perfectly horizontal or vertical, our eyes would notice the dots much too easily.

They assigned different angles to the other colors. The magenta plate is screened at 75 degrees and cyan at 105 degrees. This gives a good separation of 30 degrees between each color.

They then ran into a problem. The next angle at a 30-degree increment is 135 degrees, which is actually the same as 45 degrees (180 degrees minus 135 equals 45 degrees). So they used 90 degrees for the yellow plate. Because yellow is such a subtle color, it is less likely to cause moiré patterns even though it has only a 15-degree difference from the cyan plate.

These screen angles are not the only ones used—some companies have found their imagesetters work better with a different set of angles. However, the most important thing to remember is that each plate must have its own distinct angle.

The screen angles for cyan, magenta, yellow and black and how they combine together.

Tints of process colors

A **tint** is a percentage of a color. For example, 75 percent black is called a tint. This means that you are **screening** the black ink to display only 75 percent of the black plate. The amount of the tint on your screen is directly translated to the percentage of ink on the press: If you use a 20 percent tint of yellow on the screen, it will print as 20 percent of yellow ink on the press.

If you create a color based on a combination of two process inks, you need to do a little math to find the actual values that are printed. Let's say you create a Lavender color with 28 percent cyan and 48 percent magenta. If you make a 50 percent tint of this Lavender, the actual colors would be 14 percent cyan and 24 percent magenta.

Most software lets you create tints of process colors by first choosing the color from the color list and then choosing the tint value from various menus or palettes.

You can also define a tint of a previously created color. You can apply this tint directly from the color palette. If you change the *original* color, the *tint* changes to a tint of the new color. This is incredibly handy. Let's say you have headlines throughout your newsletter in maroon, and you've used a tint of maroon for the graphics. Your boss tells you to change the color from maroon to blue. Instead of having to change every item that had that maroon tint applied to it, you change the original color to blue, and all the tints are now tints of blue.

Adding up the inks

When you define colors using process inks, you are actually sending instructions about how much ink to put on the paper. As a general rule, you don't want to create areas with 300 percent or more of all the inks combined.

For instance, there is extremely little difference between a dark brown made from 80:100:100:30 and a dark brown made from 70:80:70:30. The first dark brown results in 310 percent ink in one area; the second brown only has 250 percent. Keeping the amount of ink under 300 percent will make your job print better and allow the paper to dry faster.

4-color black and other colors

Some designers like to add a certain amount of cyan, magenta, and yellow to the process black to make a color that is richer than the single black process ink. This black is often called a **rich black**. But you would never want to make a black color with 100 percent of all four colors (100:100:100:100). This would make a very muddy mess.

There are many different recipes for rich black. When I was in advertising, we had three formulas. The first was a neutral rich black which added 40 percent cyan and 40 percent magenta added to 100 percent black.

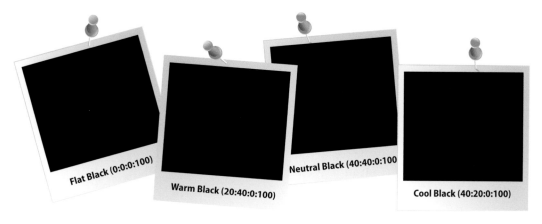

Flat Black (0:0:0:100)

Warm Black (20:40:0:100)

Neutral Black (40:40:0:100)

Cool Black (40:20:0:100)

Look carefully and you'll see the differences between the blacks in this illustration. Can you feel how one black seems warmer or cooler than the others? Do you see how the flat black is less rich than the neutral rich black?

We also created a warm black, which was 40 percent magenta and 20 percent cyan. This created a black that had a reddish hue or "warmer" color.

Finally, we had a cool black, which was 40 percent cyan and 20 percent magenta. This created a black with a blue hue or "cooler" color. If you want to make a rich black, ask your print shop what recipe they recommend.

Matching 4-color black

Another reason to define a rich black is to match the 4-color black that is in a photograph. Consider the image of the fireworks on the next page. If I need some text in a black background next to the photo, I want that black to match the color of the photo.

I define a 4-color black in my page layout program and use that color next to the photo. It may not be an exact match. But it's better than putting a "flat black" next to the photo.

The text next to the image on the left has a rich black that blends into the photo. The text on the right is a flat black that changes abruptly next to the photo.

The color "registration"

Most desktop publishing programs, especially page layout and vector drawing programs, have a color called **registration**. Registration may look like a plain ol' black on the screen, but its hidden secret is that during separations it prints on every one of the plates. So that's like having a color that is 100:100:100:100. That's 400 percent of the inks.

As I explained on page 134, anything over 300 percent of the inks is too dense to print correctly. For this reason, never use the registration color for art, images, or text in the document. Use it for things like crop marks, fold marks, or notes about the document that you want to appear on all the plates.

What is white?

Unlike painting a room, when it comes to process colors, white isn't really a color at all. It is simply the absence of the four process inks. So, if you specify a headline to be white, what you're really saying is that you don't want any ink to appear in that spot.

Now if the white headline is over the blank page what you'll get is nothing. No ink on the paper equals nothing.

If the white headline is over a picture or a colored background, it will appear as if there is white, but the reality is you're looking at the plain paper. Using white as a color doesn't add ink to the page, it actually takes away all the ink. A technical term for this is a **knockout**.

Process color projects

You may need to go outside your office to complete some of these projects. If so, make sure you get a signed permission slip.

Project #1

With a strong magnifying glass (a printer's **loupe** is excellent), examine the colors in a magazine such as *Time* or *Newsweek*. Look at the dots in the colors. Try to see the dot patterns.

Project #2

Examine the colors in a newspaper such as USA *Today*. Can you see the dots that make up the colors without using a magnifying glass at all? Are the dots in this project larger than the dots in the first project? That's the difference in the size of the linescreen.

Project #3

Find an ad that appears in a magazine as well as in a newspaper. Can you see any differences in how the colors appear? The newspaper may not able to print the colors the same way as the magazine can.

Project #4

Go visit a local print shop and ask them to show you the separations for some of their old jobs.

Project #5

Open a CYMK image in Adobe Photoshop and look at the Channels palette. See how turning on and off the different channels for cyan, magenta, yellow, and black affects the image. And see how the combinations of two and three channels appear. (This project can't be done in Photoshop Elements as that program only opens files in the RGB mode.)

Color quiz

This quiz is meant to help you learn to think in process inks. Without looking at software or a color process guide, match the CMYK values to the color you think they probably create. Cover the answers below to make sure you don't cheat.

You can also use the color palette in any graphics program (type in the CMYK values) to see how those colors actually appear.

1.	5:10:30:5	a.	orange
2.	80:0:40:0	b.	pale pink
3.	70:60:60:10	c.	dark gray
4.	0:100:100:0	d.	red
5.	0:70:100:0	e.	teal
6.	80:100:30:0	f.	dark purple
7.	10:30:20:0	g.	tan
8.	70:35:20:20	h.	light purple
9.	30:10:95:5	i.	chartreuse green
10.	25:40:0:0	j.	gun metal blue

Color quiz answers

1. g, 2. e, 3. c, 4. d, 5. a, 6. f, 7. b, 8. j, 9. i, 10. h

Spot Colors and Duotones

The previous chapter was all about process colors, the four transparent inks that combine to make full-color images on paper. Process color printing is expensive, and most projects either can't afford it or don't really need it. But what if you want some color on the page? That's when you use a **spot color**, just an ink or two applied to text or graphics that adds bright spots to your page.

Spot colors are one of the most misunderstood aspects of printing. Part of the problem is that many designers, print shops, and software companies use a variety of terms to describe spot colors: specialty, Pantone, custom, flat, solid, second color, and fifth or sixth colors are just some of the terms used to describe the technique.

Whatever you call them, spot colors can help you create many special effects in your printed projects, including **duotones**, and they can also help lower the printing costs.

Why use spot colors?

The term **spot color** refers to any other single color besides the four process colors (cyan, magenta, yellow, or black) that is printed on paper. The print shop always has black ink on the press, so they typically only charge you for colors besides black because then they have to wash the press to put new colors on. (*For more information on the number of colors used for printing, see Chapter 11.*)

Some print jobs use both spot and process colors. A typical project might use process colors for most of the text and photos, and spot colors for special areas of the project, like where you want a metallic color or a richer red than the red that's created with CMYK colors. But let's look at the different uses for spot color.

Saving money

If you want to put color into your project but can't justify the expense of the four-color process, use a spot color. This book uses process colors to add color to the pages. That means my publisher has to pay for four-color printing.

But if my publisher had wanted to save money, they could have printed the book using black ink plus a spot color. That second color would add some variety without costing as much as a four-color printing.

Color matching

One reason to use a spot color is to match a specific color. For example, it's very common to match the colors used in company logos. The red used by Coca-Cola is a spot color. The American Express Card green is a spot color. The MasterCard orange-and-yellow logo are two spot colors.

Color matching is why spot colors are sometimes called **specialty** or **custom colors**, colors that are specifically mixed for a company or a project.

Metallic effects

Another reason to use spot color is to create a special effect, such as silver or gold metal. You might use metallic ink or special metallic foils. There's no way the ordinary process inks can create that metallic look, so whenever you see it, you know the press used a spot color.

Fluorescent effects

You can also use fluorescent spot colors to make the images in a printed piece seem to glow or shine from the page. Fluorescent inks have special chemicals added. The yellow and orange colors on a box of Tide detergent are examples of fluorescent spot colors. Many magazines print their covers with fluorescent colors to call attention to the magazine on the newsstand. Book covers use fluorescent spot color to make the title of the book jump from the shelf. Whenever you see printing that seems to glow, you know the project was printed using a spot color.

Many times fluorescent and metallic colors are used in jobs printed with process colors. This means the job is printed with more than four colors. When spot colors are added to a project that already uses process colors, the spot colors are said to be the **fifth or sixth colors**.

Small text

Another reason to use spot colors is to help avoid **registration issues** when dealing with very small text. For instance, let's say you want a lot of body text in a color such as green. If the green comes from two process colors (cyan and yellow), small text could look a little fuzzy if the plates don't match exactly. (*See Chapter 15 for an example of what that looks like.*) Instead of two process colors, using a single spot color green plate avoids the problem of getting the colors to register exactly.

You can find a lot of this technique in textbooks, especially for teacher editions, which have lots of colored text in the margins.

"No-color" colors

Spot color doesn't have to be an actual color—the "spot" can be a special printing effect. For instance, a **varnish** is a printed coat of shellac or plastic. It might cover the entire surface of the page or just a specific area. You've probably seen spot varnish, where an area on a page looks very shiny compared to the rest of the page or cover. That varnish is specified by a spot color.

Embossing is a technique where text or an image is pressed into the printed page to create a raised surface. This is also specified as a spot color, even though embossing doesn't add any actual ink to the page .

Defining spot colors

It's actually very easy to define a spot color. Instead of choosing the process color setting in your color editor, you just set the color type as spot color.

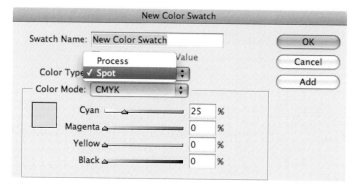

The easiest way to define a spot color is to simply choose the Spot designation.

Once you define the spot color, an indicator appears next to the color name that shows it is not a process color.

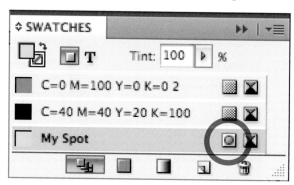

The circle inside the square next to the color name indicates that the color is defined as a spot color.

When you create a spot color, like process colors, it too will have a screen angle. Fortunately you don't have to worry about setting

A Spot Color by Any Other Name

The most common confusion when creating spot colors is what to call them. The most important thing is that if you create the same color in two different programs, you must give the color the exact same name! For instance, if you name a spot color "My Spot" in one program, and then name it "my spot" in another, you actually have defined two colors that will separate onto two plates.

This means if you create a spot color in your page layout program, and the same color in an illustration program, the two color names must match exactly. That includes spelling, spaces, and capitalizations.

the screen angles for spot colors unless you are going to mix them in a duotone (*covered on page 146*). If you do create a duotone that mixes black and a spot color, you may need to talk to your print shop for the best way to set the screen angle.

Using spot color guides

Spot colors can be difficult to print on the office inkjet printer. With only four cartridges in the printer, it is difficult — if not impossible — to replicate a corporate spot color. This can be a problem when you want to show a proof of the project to a client.

Use a guide, not the screen

Each of the spot color companies has created books that show how their spot colors look in print. In addition, spot color companies provide software for desktop publishing applications that allows you to pick from their libraries of colors within the program. These spot colors correspond to the colors that are printed in the spot color guides. Instead of relying on the color from the inkjet printer, you can show the client the actual spot color swatch in the color guide.

Don't create a color on the screen and expect that color to appear on the printed page. It just won't happen. You can calibrate your screen (set the colors to an industry standard) with software, and that will help coordinate the colors you see on your screen with other calibrated monitors. But it still does not ensure that the ink on the paper is exactly what you see on the screen.

But don't worry if the color on your screen doesn't match the printed book! *It doesn't matter what it looks like on your screen—what matters is that it will print that color.*

Spot color effects

Once you start working with spot colors, you'll discover there are many special effects you can create using just two inks to arrive at at different looks. Some of these effects are very simple to achieve; others need specialized software. The following are just some effects you can create with spot colors.

Tints

Once you have defined a spot color, you can then make a tint of it. This simply means that instead of using the color at 100 percent, you use it at a certain percentage of its value, such as 10 percent. The press prints tiny dots of ink; these tiny dots mix with the white background of the paper to give the appearance of a lighter color.

Mixing inks

It's very easy to tint a spot color to make it lighter. But how do you make a spot color darker? How can you add black to the spot color? Mixing a spot color and black is a special technique called **Mixed Inks** in InDesign and **Multi-Inks** in QuarkXPress. With Mixed Inks you can create a wider range of colors on your page than with just the spot color and its tints.

Overprinting

Ordinarily in a layout, if one item is on top of another, the portion of the bottom item does not print where it's hidden beneath the top one. The top is said to **knockout** the bottom. But if the top **overprints**, the bottom object prints even where it is beneath the top one. This means the ink from the top item combines with the ink for the bottom item, which causes the colors of two objects to mix together.

Overprinting allows you to combine spot colors together. For instance, you need to set a varnish color to overprint the images below. This allows the images to be seen under the varnish plate. If you don't set the varnish to overprint, it will delete the image underneath.

Overprinting is used with both spot as well as process colors. For an example of overprinting, see Chapter 19.

Colorizing photos

You can also use spot colors to change the look of photographs. The easiest way to do this is to change the black of a photograph to a spot color, as shown below. This is sometimes called **colorizing** the photo.

An example of tinting a grayscale image. Here the black color of the left image has been changed to the magenta plate. It's a very simple way to colorize a photo.

To colorize a photo in a page layout application, you need to import a grayscale image. Once you have put the image on the page layout page, you can colorize it—just select the image and choose a color from the color palette. This changes all the black pixels in the image to a different color.

Spotting spot colors

Sometimes it helps to understand the different effects you can create with spot colors if you know when spot colors have been used. Look at different printed materials and try to find the spot colors. It's easy to pick them out when they're fluorescent or metallic colors, but they're a little harder to identify if four different colors have been used.

One quick way to tell if a color is spot or process is to look for the dot pattern that is created by the four-color process. If you see a dot pattern in a color, it is most likely a process ink. If a color such as a light orange or green is solid (no dots), then it is most likely a spot color.

A simulation of what spot colors look like under a magnifying glass. A solid area of color or a single color of dots (left and middle examples) indicates the color is a spot color. A pattern of dots of any of the process colors (shown on the right as magenta and yellow) indicate a process color.

Duotones

Even though a grayscale photograph can display up to 256 levels of gray on a monitor, a printing press can only reproduce about 50 levels of gray. In two-color printing, you can print a grayscale photograph as a **duotone**, a special process that allows you to mix two different colors together in a photo, each color capable of 50 levels, which can significantly increase the depth of the image.

You can also make **tritones** using three colors and **quadtones** using four colors.

Duotones in Photoshop

Today, the most sophisticated way to make a true duotone is to use the patented technology in Adobe Photoshop. You choose the two inks you want to use in the duotone, typically black and a spot color. You adjust the "curves" of each of the colors, which changes the amount of ink that prints. This essentially creates the two versions of the halftone screen that are necessary to print a duotone.

Adjusting the curves for a duotone is not a foolproof process. Some spot colors, such as light yellows, require different settings than, say, dark browns. Different images also require different settings than others; for instance, a human face would use different curves than a shiny metal teapot. If you are in doubt as to how to adjust the curves, talk to the commercial print shop. They will be able to advise you on the best settings for your image.

The fake duotone on the left was created by taking a grayscale photo and adding a cyan background behind the black plate. It looks dull and flat compared to the true duotone, created in Photoshop, on the right.

You can also use the duotone controls to add one of the process colors to a grayscale image. The duotone above is an example of adding the process color cyan to a black and white image.

Fake duotones

If you don't want to (or can't) use Photoshop to create a true duotone with different images for each color, you can still create a fake duotone by placing a grayscale image over a tint of a color. However, these fake duotones are not as interesting as creating a proper duotone in Photoshop.

Spot color projects

Don't worry about finishing these projects quickly. These projects are suggested as a way to look at printed materials with a spot color eye.

Project #1

Examine the envelopes that you get from direct mail companies. Look for those printed with black and another color. When you see only two colors on the envelope, most likely it is a spot color.

Project #2

Go visit a magazine stand and look for magazines that have bright orange or another neon color on the cover. That neon color is usually a spot color. (Don't stand there reading the magazine if you're not going to buy it!)

Project #3

Go to a bookstore and look at some of the covers for the gothic novels or science fiction paperbacks. See if you can find examples of varnish, metallic inks, or embossing on the covers.

Project #4

Go to the laundry detergent aisle of your supermarket. Look at the boxes of detergents. See all those glowing colors? (You may need your sunglasses.) Those are fluorescent spot colors.

Project #5

Find some take-out menus from a local pizza place or Chinese restaurant. Count the number of colors. Is the menu printed with two or four colors? If it is only two colors, most likely the restaurant saved money by printing black plus a spot color. (The Chinese restaurant in my neighborhood uses black plus a spot color for its menus as well as the covers for the chopsticks.

How Many Colors to Print

One of the most important decisions you have to make about a print job is how many colors to print. You need to know how many colors you can work with *before* you start creating images and laying out text and graphics.

This decision is based on which type of color inks you plan to use: process, spot, or both.

Number of colors on a printing press

The number of *colors* on a printing press refers to how many *inks* are applied to the paper. It might be a full-color job, but it's printed (*as you learned in Chapter 9*) with four inks. Each ink counts as a color. As a general rule, the more colors in the document, the more it costs to print.

One-color printing

One-color printing is the cheapest type of printing you can get. There is only one printing plate, which uses only one ink. Most people use black ink for one-color jobs, but you can also have the print shop use a spot color instead of black. If you do use a color instead of black, the print shop may charge you a small wash-up fee to clean off the special color ink after they are finished printing your job.

Don't change your electronic files from black to a special color for one-color printing! Just tell the print shop that the black text and graphics (the black "plate") should actually be printed using your chosen color, and they will put a different color ink on the press.

If you use a desktop color printer to output the document in color—perhaps to show a client what it looks like in color—all the color prints onto one page and it doesn't really matter how many colors you have chosen in the file. But if you plan to take the document somewhere else for final output, make sure the color has been defined as a spot color. If not, the color will separate into the separate CMYK components when you send it to the service bureau or print shop for final output.

Two-color printing

Two-color printing is more expensive than one-color. Most two-color printing uses black plus a second color, which might be a spot color or one of the process inks. However, you can use any combination of two inks—you can print black and process cyan, black and spot green, spot green and spot purple, process magenta and spot yellow, or any other combination of two inks. (Remember, the paper color doesn't count—you get that color free.)

Once you have chosen to work with two colors, you should consider how those two colors might combine. For instance, a tint of a spot green could be combined with a tint of a spot purple to create the look of a third color, brown (*see Chapter 10 for descriptions of tinted colors*).

Before you decide to mix tints of spot colors, talk to the print shop that will be printing the job. They have the best idea as to what tints of which colors mix well together, and they probably have sample books that show you what to expect when certain inks hit certain papers.

Consider the Paper Color.

As you work, keep in mind that the paper color is not considered one of the "colors" of the job. If the ink is black and the paper is pink, the job is still considered a one-color job because it uses only one color of ink.

The color of the paper affects the appearance of the color of the ink. Green ink will look different on pink paper than it will on brown paper. Choose ink and paper colors accordingly.

Three-color printing

You rarely hear of projects printed with three colors; this is because of the way colors are printed. If you have a one-color job, the shop will typically use a printing press with one ink roller and one plate. A two-color job uses a press with two rollers and two sets of plates. But there is no **three-color press**—the next size up is a four-color press with four rollers and four plates for four inks. Choosing a four-color press is significantly more expensive than choosing a two-color press, but if you have a project that needs three colors, it's most likely going to print on a four-color press. As long as you're paying for the use of the four-color press, you might as well add the extra color. So printing almost always jumps from two to four colors.

Four-color printing

A **four-color press** using process inks (*CMYK; see Chapter 9*) is the most common printing solution for magazines, direct mail brochures, catalogs, greeting cards, color postcards, and so on. It's rather easy to identify four-color process printing—as soon as you see a photograph printed in color, you know the job was printed in at least four colors.

Because most four-color printing uses process inks, it's often called **four-color process printing**. Cyan, magenta, yellow, and black inks combine to create all the other colors. However, that doesn't mean that all four-color printing is process—you can use any combination of colors on a four-color press. For example, you might choose to combine black and three spot colors. The options on a four-color press give you more flexibility in creating specific colors or special effects with metallic colors. The packages for many bars of soap or toothpastes are printed with four spot colors. That's how they get the special metallic colors. But if you see a photograph on the box, then those are process colors.

Six-color printing

Six-color printing, as you probably suspect, is even more expensive than four-color. Most six-color printing is used for packaging where the four process colors are combined with two more spot colors. (In case you were wondering, five-color printing is the same as three-color printing in that as long as you're on a six-color press, you might as well get your money's worth and use all six colors.) With six-color printing, a package can show a full-color photo and also use a special color that matches the company's logo. Cereal boxes are an excellent example of six-color printing—they use the four process colors to print the mouth-watering bowl of cereal with fruit and milk, and they also use two spot colors to print the logo or the name of the company in its own special colors.

Some very expensive brochures, such as those for new cars, are also printed in six colors. This lets the designer display the car in a full-color photo, as well as add text or graphics in silver or gold. For some brochures the sixth color is not a color, but a varnish applied over an image to make that image stand out more. (*For more on spot colors, see Chapter 10.*)

High-fidelity printing

Another type of six-color printing is called **high-fidelity printing** (often referred to as **hifi** printing). Hifi printing is a result of the fact that the four process inks don't always capture the complete range of colors in photographs. So instead of limiting the printing of photographs to just four colors, hifi printing adds two more colors to the mix. With six inks, there is a wider range of colors possible in photographs. Hifi printing is said to have a wider gamut of colors.

One brand of hifi printing, **Hexachrome®**, is from the Pantone company. Hexachrome adds orange and green inks to the mix of process colors. These two inks help make flesh tones and the vast variety of greens in the world look closer to their original colors. Some software packages, such as InDesign and QuarkXPress, allow you to define colors using the Hexachrome system. If you want to use hifi colors, make sure your print shop can recreate them, and ask about how you should prepare any scanned images.

Separations

When you print in color, you want to make sure that the correct number of *separations* are created for the press (*see Chapter 9 for an explanation of separations*). You definitely don't want to have more separations come out of the printer than the number of colors you had planned to use. For instance, if you planned and budgeted for a two-color job, you had better make sure your file only prints two separations. If it doesn't, fixing the problem at the service bureau or print shop will cost time and money you may not have expected to spend.

Paper separations

When I first started working with computer graphics, the only way to avoid problems was to make what was called **paper separations**: Before we sent the file to the service bureau, we opened the print dialog box and choose "Make Separations" and then counted the number of pieces of paper that came out of the printer. There would be a piece of paper for each plate; four for process color printing, two for a two-color job; one for a one-color job. Of course, all of the separations would print only in the black toner.

Onscreen separations

These days it is much easier (and saves tons of trees) to just use the electronic separation features that are built into programs such as Adobe Acrobat and InDesign. Instead of counting sheets of paper, you can just turn on and off the indicators for each of the plates to keep an eye on how the page will separate. (I love doing this to see how the process colors combine.)

In InDesign, you open the Separations Preview panel and turn on the setting for Separations. Each of the process colors will be listed as well as any spot colors that may be in the document. You then click the eyeball controls to view each of the color plates.

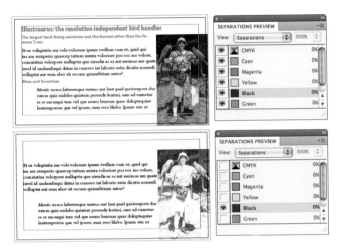

The Separations Preview panel in InDesign shows the color plates on a page. Here the top image shows the four process colors plus a fifth spot color. The bottom image shows just the black plate.

In Acrobat, you choose the Output Preview command from the Print Production area. You use the check boxes to control the display of the various color plates. The panel also lets you change the display of black and the paper colors. With these electronic separations, you should be able to avoid any unexpected separations when your job goes to press.

The Output Preview panel in Acrobat shows the color plates as well as additional prepress information. Here the black and cyan plates are shown.

Counting color projects

You shouldn't be in a rush to finish these projects. They are an unending journey of examining all printed material to see how the colors are printed.

Project #1

Find examples of one-color printing. What color is usually used?

Project #2

Find examples of one-color printing that don't use black. Look for any photographs in those examples. Do they look good or not? If not, why not?

Project #3

Find examples of two-color printing. How many use black as the primary color and a spot color as the second?

Project #4

Look at the colors on a soda can. Is there any white on the can? What color is the can itself? Given that the can itself is not white, how did the white area get on the can? Can you find other examples where white is added as a spot color?

Project #5

Examine the colors printed on a cereal box. Open up the flaps of the box (take the cereal out first) and look for squares of colors. If the cereal box was printed with just four colors, there will be just four squares. If the box was printed with six colors, there will be six squares —four process colors and two spot colors.

5467169 04/08

092241

An example of the color bars found on the sides of a package. Notice the extra colors of green and dark blue.

Project #6

If you find a package printed with six colors, try to see where the extra two spot colors were used. Hint: Most likely the extra two colors are used for a company logo or name of the product.

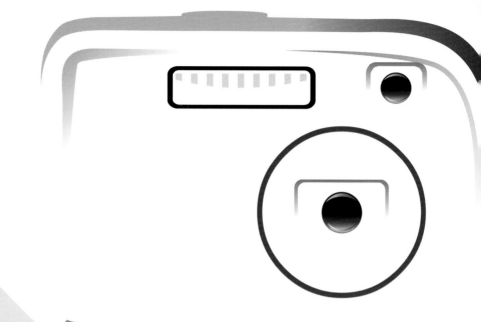

▶ GETTING STUFF INTO THE COMPUTER

The key to making your projects look good when they come out of the computer is making sure they look good when they go into the computer. Here are tips for getting images and typefaces into the computer correctly.

"Things should be as simple as possible, but not simpler."

ALBERT EINSTEIN

Digital Cameras

At first, digital cameras were limited to only professional photographers working in studios. However, as the technology developed (and prices dropped) digital cameras became popular, not just with professional photographers, but with consumers as well.

Today, it's hard to find anyone who doesn't own some type of digital camera. It may be a simple point-and-shoot camera that slips into a shirt pocket. It may be a sophisticated SLR camera that can take a wide variety of lenses. Or it could just be the tiny camera built into a cell phone.

What makes digital cameras so useful is that the images can be quickly transferred into a computer, viewed instantly on the monitor, adjusted electronically, and then placed into an electronic layout.

How digital cameras work

If you're old enough to remember film cameras, you probably know that those cameras captured images by opening a small hole (called an aperture) and letting light into the camera. The light then focused onto the camera film which captured the image with a chemical reaction.

Digital cameras substitute an electronic image sensor for film. The electronic sensor passes the light onto individual pixels for each of the red, green, and blue colors in the light. If this seems similar to the description of RGB images covered back in Chapter 5, it's

because they are the same. The images created by digital cameras are captured as RGB files.

Some digital cameras store their images on small electronic cards that can be removed from the camera. Other cameras store their images on internal hard disks that can't be removed. This affects how many images you can store on the camera before they need to be transferred to a computer. For instance, if you fill up an electronic card, you can just swap it out for an empty one. If the camera stores images on an internal hard disk you will need to remove the images when the camera is full.

From camera to computer

There are many different ways to get the images from your digital camera into the computer. You can attach a cable from the camera to the computer. You can take the card out of the camera and use an image adapter to plug it into the computer. You can use email to send the image to yourself or others. Finally, there are even ways to automatically transfer each photo as you click the shutter using a **bluetooth** or a wifi network.

It doesn't matter what method you choose. Once your images are in the computer, you have all the features of image editing applications to modify the photos. You can convert the files to CMYK and then add them to your page layout program for publishing.

Types of digital cameras

There are no hard-and-fast rules for these categories of cameras. What may seem like a professional camera to one person will seem less to another.

Professional digital cameras

The most common professional digital cameras are the **single lens reflex** (SLR) digital cameras. These cameras look similar to traditional 35mm cameras. The single lens of these cameras refers to the single lens that is used to both compose the shot as well as let light into the camera. Then, as you press the shutter control, a mirror inside the camera body flips and instead of the light going into the viewfinder, the light is sent directly to the back of the camera. Professional photographers feel that the single lens is a more accurate view of how the final image will look.

As any professional photographer will tell you, the most important part of a camera is its lens. The professional SLR cameras all have the ability to swap out one type of lens for another. This is what makes those cameras so professional. You can exchange a telephoto lens that shoots long distances with a macro lens for closeup work. Most professional photographers will have two or three lenses that they swap on a camera.

An example of a professional single lens reflex camera with exchangeable lenses.

Here are some of the other features that are necessary for a camera to be considered of professional quality:

- ▶ **Aperture control**. The aperture is the opening that allows light into the camera. Professional cameras allow you to control the aperture manually.

- ▶ **Shutter speed**. When the aperture opens to let light into the camera, it closes after a certain amount of time. The longer the aperture stays open, the more light enters the camera. Professionals manually adjust the shutter speed to let more or less light in.

▶ Working with **depth of field**. The depth of field is the range of distance within which objects appear to be in focus. Professional cameras use a combination of the aperture and the length of the camera lens to control the depth of field.

▶ **Bracketing images.** Most photographers don't rely on just one setting for shutter speed and aperture. So they use a technique called bracketing where they take three pictures of the image at the same time with one click. One image is adjusted to be slightly underexposed, one is slightly overexposed, and the other is normal. These three images allow the photographer more choices for the final shot.

▶ **Additional file formats**. In addition to the common JPEG file format, most professional cameras allow you to save your images as RAW files. Unlike JPEG files that apply a slight amount of compression, RAW files are captured with no compression or other enhancements. They are considered the most pure form of the image you can work with. However, RAW files must be processed into other formats to be used in page layouts.

These are the most basic features for professional cameras. However, don't let the word *professional* fool you. I know plenty of people who insist on buying a professional camera, but they then turn on all the automatic controls and just point and click. They may own a professional camera, but they use it in a most unprofessional manner.

Studio Cameras

Single lens cameras are portable; that is, even with a long telephoto lens, you can still carry them around. But there is another type of camera called a studio camera. They have much larger image sensor areas which make them much bigger than the typical SLR camera. This means they take very high quality images, but are way too big to tote around. And even then, they work by taking three separate shots of an image — one for each color channel. This means that the subject of the photograph can't move, which makes them great for still life photos, but not for portraits.

Consumer digital cameras

Lower-priced digital cameras are consumer digital cameras, which are sometimes called point-and-shoot cameras. These cameras are much smaller than professional SLR cameras and can easily be carried in a shirt pocket.

An example of a consumer digital camera. Notice the fixed lens and small, compact size.

The two main differences between these cameras and SLR ones is that the consumer cameras have one lens that is not removable. Also, they have a separate viewfinder from the actual camera lens.

What these cameras lack in sophisticated lenses, they make up with special features that make the cameras incredibly easy to use. These include automatic focusing, exposure controls, and image stabilizing. These cameras also let you take very simple videos complete with sound.

Point-and-shoot cameras are excellent for capturing images for Web pages, for printing on photographic-quality inkjet printers, adding images to video presentations, or for projects that will be output to desktop printers and reproduced on copy machines.

Prosumer Cameras

Somewhere between high-end SLR cameras and low-end point-and-shoot digital cameras are the **prosumer** (professional + consumer) cameras. They are also labeled for the "serious amateur," which is easier to find than a sloppy professional.

Priced a little bit higher than a low-end camera, but less than a professional camera, prosumer cameras are usually SLR cameras that may not have lenses that can be swapped. You won't necessarily find these cameras labeled as prosumer. You will know them by their price.

There are some instances where consumer digital cameras can be used for journalism or even advertising. However, you should understand how they work before you try to use them for your own print projects.

Camera phones

It's hard to find a cell phone that doesn't have a camera built into it. Does that mean that there is no need for digital cameras? Can't everyone just use their cell phones to take pictures for advertising or publishing? Hardly! Even though some of the newer camera phones have very high resolutions, their camera sensors aren't high quality, and their lenses are too primitive to take excellent pictures. You wouldn't even want to trust your family holiday photos to the camera in your cell phone.

So what good are they? They are spur-of-the-moment memory savers. For instance, if you're looking for a new house, they are an excellent way to record the layout of each room. And because the images are often tied to email, they can be easily sent to your spouse for his or her approval.

Resolution of digital cameras

Once you've decided on the type of digital camera, the next consideration is resolution. This is expressed as the total number of pixels in the area that is captured. For instance, if the area that is captured is 3,000 pixels across by 2,000 pixels down, the total

The Missing Megapixels

You can't go by the actual number of megapixels listed for a camera to get the final output. For instance, my iPhone takes an image that is 1600 pixels by 1200 pixels. That's a total of 1,920,000 pixels. But Apple (and every other digital camera company) calls this amount a 2.1 megapixel camera. What happened to the missing pixels?

The difference isn't some sort of mathematic oddity. It comes from the fact that there are pixels in the image sensor that handle the electronics of the circuits. So, strictly speaking there are more than two million pixels in the camera. It's just that not all of them contribute to the final resolution of the image.

Megapixels or Megabytes?

Here's the part that always gets me confused. Let's say I take a photo with a 6 megapixel camera. That's six million pixels in the image. But when I open that file in Photoshop, it lists the image as 17.2M. Shouldn't the number be 6M?

Well, the first thing to realize is that 17.2M stands for 17.2 *megabytes*, not megapixels. A megabyte is the size of the space on a disk that is needed to store the image. And while I can't explain all the math here, 1 pixel does not exactly equal 1 byte. It's close, but not exact. In fact, 6 megapixels actually comes out to 5.72 megabytes.

So why then is the image size not displayed as 5.72M? Well, remember, the image is stored with three separate channels of information: red, green, and blue. So that triples the 5.72 megabytes, which comes out to 17.2 megabytes. But what's more important to remember is that the original resolution is still 3,000 pixels across, and 2,000 pixels down.

---

number of pixels is 6,000,000 pixels. Every million pixels is called a **megapixel.** So six million pixels is 6 megapixels.

Once these pixels have been captured, the pixels-per-inch (PPI) value can be changed, depending on how you plan to use the images (*see Chapter 6 to understand how the print area of an image changes as the resolution changes*).

It was only a few years back when the top resolution for a professional digital camera was 6 megapixels. Today, you can find camera phones with 12.1 megapixels! However, resolution doesn't always indicate a good output. You also need to look at the type of image sensors.

Types of image sensors

There are two types of image sensors that are used in digital cameras. Most use a **charged coupling device** (CCD). Others use a

---

Grayscale Digital Cameras?

Growing up, I always had to choose between loading my camera with black-and-white or color film. But today there aren't any grayscale digital cameras. When I want grayscale images, I convert the RGB image into a grayscale equivalent using an image editing program.

---

complementary metal oxide semiconductor (CMOS). You don't have to learn the physics behind each type of sensor. Just know that each type has its pros and cons.

▶ **CCD sensors create higher-quality images with less noise in the image.** (Noise is the term used for pixels that are in an image that shouldn't be there. These noisy pixels tend to make the image look splotchy.) CMOS sensors are more likely to have areas with visible noise.

▶ **CMOS sensors are more energy efficient and use less power.** They are better for cameras that have smaller batteries.

▶ **CMOS sensors are less expensive than CCD ones.** This makes CMOS sensors popular for cheaper cameras.

▶ **CCD sensors have higher-quality pixels** and can pack more of them in a smaller area.

File size and compression

Just because a camera comes with 12 megapixels doesn't mean you have to save your work with all 12 million pixels. Most cameras let you choose to shoot your images at lower resolutions. If I know I will only be using my photos as demo images on screen, I usually lower the resolution of the images in the camera. This lets me save more images onto the camera's storage card.

Digital cameras also let you save your files in different file formats. Professional cameras use lossless formats (*see page 114*) such as TIFF or RAW that do not change the quality or details in the file. These formats take up more room in the camera, but provide the highest quality in the image.

High-end cameras also let you save as JPEG files with very low compression. This the quality of the image very slightly.

Consumer digital cameras generally save their images only as JPEG files. These cameras usually let you choose the quality setting for the image with the labels: good, better, or best. The best quality applies the least amount of compression; better quality applies a little more compression; and good applies the greatest amount of compression.

Viewing and sorting digital images

If you've ever been on a professional photo shoot, you know that photographers don't just point and click to take one photo. They click, click, click to take hundreds of photos to cover every conceivable angle, view, and exposure. After the shoot, it is a chore to wade through hundreds of files to find the good ones.

Traditional contact sheets and lightboxes

When photographers took 35 MM photos, they needed a way to view hundreds of photos without developing each picture on a separate piece of photographic paper. The photographers would place strips of developed film on a piece of photographic paper. The paper was then exposed to light.

An example of how a portion of a contact sheet of images would appear. A magnifying glass was required to view the images.

When the paper was developed, the photos were displayed as a series of small images inside the panels of the film. (The term contact sheet came from how the negative was in **contact** with the photographic paper.) The photographer and client would use a magnifying glass to view the images on the paper and mark the ones they liked.

Photographers would also arrange individual 35 mm slides on special types of lamps, called **lightboxes**, that allowed light to pass through the slides. They would again use magnifying glasses to view and choose the images they liked.

Digital contact sheets and lightboxes

With digital cameras, it's very easy to take thousands of photographs without changing the image card. Fortunately, there are software applications that work like the traditional contact sheets and lightboxes. These applications let you view, sort, arrange, adjust, and edit digital images without opening hundreds of files.

Adobe® Bridge®, Adobe® Photoshop® Lightroom®, Apple® iPhoto®, and Apple® Apperture® all allow you to easily sort through hundreds of images. iPhoto is the most basic product. Bridge comes with any of the Adobe applications. Lightroom and Apperture are professional products with very specialized controls for processing thousands of images at a time.

Adobe Bridge is an electronic version of a contact sheet or the old lightbox thats let you view, sort, adjust, and modify digital images.

Digital camera projects

These projects require using a wide variety of digital cameras. You're not expected to own all of them yourself. Find a buddy and you can both use each other's cameras.

Project #1

Find a digital camera that lets you change the amount of pixels in the image. Change the pixel size of the images from the smallest to largest. Notice how the number of pictures the camera can take changes.

Project #2

On the same camera as project #1, change the quality of the JPEG compression. Does that change how many images you can store on the camera?

Project #3

Find a high-end camera that lets you work in the RAW format. See how many images can be stored in that format.

Project #4

Find a camera phone and see if there are any controls for taking pictures. Is there a flash? Is there a focus control? Can you change how many pixels are captured? Can you change the JPEG compression? Is there anything you can do?

Project #5

Take some pictures with a camera phone. Download them to your computer and see how large they are. Then, email the photos from the camera phone to the computer. Are the emailed photos the same size as the downloaded ones? (They're not from my iPhone.)

Project #6

Go into a very low light condition. (A romantic candle-lit restaurant is fine.) Take some photos. Later on, download the images to your computer. Look at the shadow areas of the photo. Do you see any splotchy areas? That's the noise from the lower-quality image sensors.

Project #7

Take a few different digital cameras on a photo shoot. Take the same scene with the various cameras. Download the photos to your computer and compare them. Can you see the difference between the photos?

Project #8

Find a professional digital camera and examine the settings. Is there one for bracketing images? If so, take some photos using the bracketing features. Download the photos and see how bracketing affects the images.

Scanners and Scanning

A scanner is the bridge between tangible objects and digital images—a scanner allows you to capture objects outside the computer and put them inside the computer.

There are many different types of scanners and many prices—some cost just a few hundred dollars, others hundreds of thousands of dollars. No matter how much it costs, a scanner doesn't scan objects as automatically as a point-and-shoot camera; if you don't set the right settings on the scanner, you won't get good results.

Years ago, every designer I knew owned a very expensive scanner. They used them to scan prints and negatives of photographs to use in their designs.

Today, things are much different. I just got an email from a top Photoshop expert who told me he no longer uses any scanner except the one that converts his hotel and restaurant receipts to files for tax purposes. The need for scanners has dropped dramatically with the increased availability and lower prices of professional digital cameras. However, since I'm sure there are still plenty of people with a shoebox full of old images, here's a basic course in scanners and scanning.

Principles of scanners

If you've ever used a photocopy machine, you're already familiar with the basic principle of a scanner. Just like on a photocopy machine, an image is placed on a scanner surface and light passes across it. As the light hits the image or passes through, the light changes depending on what is in the image. Those changes to the light are then stored as a digital file. That digital file is called the **scan**, or the **scanned image**.

As mentioned in Chapter 2, a desktop printer also uses many of the same principles as a photocopy machine. So at a very basic level, a desktop scanner and a desktop printer are simply photocopy machines with very powerful computers in the middle to manipulate the images. In fact, you can buy a printer that also contains a scanner, just like a photocopy machine.

Almost all scanners use the same CCD image sensors found in some digital cameras. The more sensors in the scanner, the more information can be stored.

The highest-quality scanners use a technology called PMT (photo-multiplier tubes) that read the CMYK color values in the image and then translate that information into RGB data (*did you read Chapter 5 about RGB and CMYK?*). The PMT technology is found almost exclusively in professional drum scanners (*see page 177*). Unless you've got a drum scanner, your scanner is CCD, not PMT.

There are different types of scanners, which I'll talk about on pages 174–177. Choosing the right type for a project depends on the original image and what you intend to do with the image.

Scanners use RGB

Scanners capture the color information as RGB (red, green, and blue, *as we discussed in Chapter 5*). This makes perfect sense because the point of a scanner is to put the image into the computer, which displays color as RGB. Some scanning software does offer a CMYK option (*also in Chapter 5*), but the color won't be as reliable as the RGB. If you plan to output a graphic in CMYK, work on your file in RGB, then convert it to CMYK just before you place it onto a page layout page for final output. If this confuses you at all, you probably didn't read Chapter 5.

Original images

The sorts of things you can put through the scanning process can be divided into two categories: reflective art and transparent art. Some scanners can handle both types of art; other scanners are made specifically for one or the other.

▶ **Reflective art** or images are physical objects such as photographs, canvasses, paintings, or objects. The scanner captures the light as it reflects off the original.

▶ **Transparent art** or images include film, slides, acetate, etc. The scanner captures the light as it passes through the original image.

Bit-depth

The bit-depth of a scanner refers to how much color information the scanner can capture *(see Chapter 5 for detailed information on bit depths and color modes)*. A 1-bit scanner captures only line art images. An 8-bit scanner captures grayscale. A 24-bit scanner captures RGB images.

Most office desktop scanners are 30-bit, while the higher quality graphics scanners are 36-bit. This means they can capture extra information about the colors of an image. This added bit-depth about the image provides more information to use during the color and tonal correction of an image. You may not notice the added information on the screen, but the computer knows it's there and can work with it.

Scanner resolution

The **optical resolution** of a scanner refers to how much detail the scanner can capture. The optical resolution is expressed as two numbers, such as 600 x 1200 PPI. The first number, 600, is the

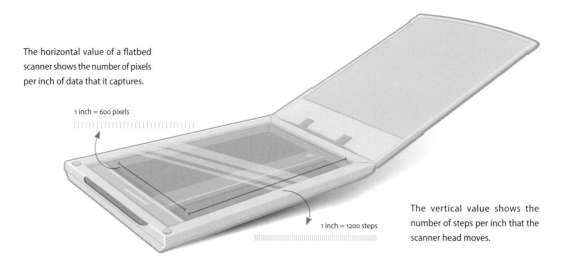

The horizontal value of a flatbed scanner shows the number of pixels per inch of data that it captures.

1 inch = 600 pixels

1 inch = 1200 steps

The vertical value shows the number of steps per inch that the scanner head moves.

number of pixels per inch of information the scanner captures in the horizontal direction. The higher the number of pixels per inch, the more detail the scanner can capture.

The second number, 1200, refers to the number of steps the scanner head moves along the vertical direction. The actual resolution of the image is only the number of pixels per inch, not the number of steps.

You may also see the resolution of a scanner expressed as the **interpolated** or **enhanced resolution**. Interpolated resolution is much higher than the optical resolution. For instance, a scanner with an optical resolution of 600 x 1200 PPI might have an interpolated resolution of 9600. This means the scanner software is able to interpolate (kind of fake) the true resolution of the image into a higher number. Interpolation doesn't actually increase the detail in an image—it just means the image can be enlarged without any obvious pixelation.

Types of scanners

Here are descriptions of the most common scanners you might use today.

Hand-held scanners

The least expensive scanners are those small ones you **hold in your hand and drag across an image**. These scanners are supposed to make it easier to go to a library and make notes of the pages that are important to you.

They are terrific items, but I don't recommend them for printing a high-quality image. For instance, if you want to show an example of an illustrated manuscript, you should *not* use a hand-held scanner to capture the image.

Sheet-fed scanners

The next level up are the sheet-fed scanners where you insert (feed) a paper image into the scanner that resembles the top of a fax machine. These machines take all sorts of paper sizes from business cards up to letter and legal text. My favorite use for my Neat Receipts sheet-fed scanner is to make copies of my hotel receipts for tax purposes. I save the scanned images as a PDF file which I can give to my accountant at the end of the year.

Some sheet-fed scanners can handle hundreds of pages of material at a time. This makes them great for converting tons of paper into electronic documents.

But I wouldn't use a sheet-fed scanner to capture an image for a professional publication. The quality just isn't there. And the fact that the paper moves over the scanner head (instead of the scanner moving over the paper) means there can be variation along the line of the scan.

Flatbed scanners

Flatbed scanners are the most common type of desktop scanners and most closely resemble the top of an office copy machine. All flatbed scanners can handle reflective art and some have adapters for transparent art.

You can even place small objects such as coins, keys, pencils, hands, etc. on the top of a flatbed scanner. This makes scanning a quick substitute for photography.

This image was created by placing a bunch of old coins and subway tokens on the scanner glass and scanning.

It used to be that you had to spend thousands of dollars to get a professional-quality flatbed scanner. Today, it's possible to get high-end results with a flatbed scanner that costs just under a hundred dollars.

Slide scanners

Slide scanners are specially made for transparent art, such as (guess!) slides. Some of these scanners only take 35mm slides; others can take many different film sizes. You can get a slide scanner attachment for many flatbeds, although it doesn't usually give as high-quality an image as a dedicated slide scanner.

Slide scanners use extremely high resolutions to provide enough detail so a 1-inch image (the slide) can be enlarged to fill a full page without the pixels becoming obvious.

As fewer photographers take pictures with film cameras, the slide scanner has become an endangered species with only rare sightings in graphic design firms.

Drum scanners

Drum scanners are the highest quality scanners. To make a drum scan, the image (photograph, canvas, illustration, fabric, etc.) is wrapped around a transparent cylinder. The cylinder rotates as the light is focused on the image.

Drum scanners can scan either reflective or transparent art, but you're limited to art that can be mounted on a cylinder. Thus you can't use a drum scanner for images in books or art mounted on stiff illustration boards.

The original drum scanners were extremely expensive machines that took up a portion of a room and needed specially trained operators. Many print shops provided drum scanning services: You took an image to the print shop and they scanned it and gave you back the image on a disk. You then could manipulate the scan and insert it into a page layout.

Although sending out for a drum scan is still common, in recent years the prices and sizes of these scanners have dropped considerably, so many large design studios now have their own drum scanners. However, it still takes a trained operator to get the best quality scans. Also, the flatbed scanners have been getting more and more sophisticated while coming way down in price, so drum scans have been relegated to extremely high-end work.

OCR software

Scanners make pictures of images; they do not read text. If you scan a page of text, like from a book or a typed letter, you'll get a *picture* of the text—you won't be able to edit, change the typeface, or search the text.

But there is special software called **Optical Character Recognition** (OCR) that is often included with scanners, or you can buy it separately to use with your existing scanner. This software recognizes the shapes of letters and creates an editable text file from the page on the scanner.

OCR software is useful for converting large amounts of printed information into editable text. Depending on the clarity of the original text, it can take some time and effort to get all of the text translated correctly. For a single sheet of text, a fast typist may be quicker and more accurate than scanning and using OCR software; for a large body of work that needs to be digitized, OCR is an incredible solution.

Preparing to scan

If you are using a flatbed scanner, there are some general principles you should follow to make sure you get the best quality scan.

- ▶ **Clean the glass**. Make sure you keep the glass of the scanner as clean as possible. Watch out for small defects — dust, scratches, and fingerprints all affect the final quality of the scan. Check the scanner documentation for the cleaning liquids and materials that are safe to use on the glass of the scanner.

- ▶ **Take care of the art**. Handle the art carefully to make sure it doesn't pick up any fingerprints, dust, scratches, etc.

- ▶ **Use glossy photos**. Photos on glossy paper make better scans than photos on matte surfaces. The matte surface has thousands of small indentations in the paper that will affect the quality of a scan. A glossy photo has a clear surface that does not change its look after it's scanned.

- ▶ **Straighten the image**. Make sure the image is as straight as possible. You can use the edge of the glass to align the photograph, but because the optical quality of the glass is better in the center, you may want to place the art in the center of the scanner. Some scanners provide pieces of cardboard to place on the glass to help give you a straight edge in the center.

  If you find your scanned image is crooked, you can straighten it in a program like Photoshop. However, don't rely on rotating an image electronically because it forces the pixels in the image to **resample** (*see page 93*), which causes a loss of detail. It is much better to scan perfectly straight, if at all possible.

▶ **Keep the image on the glass**. Put the top of the scanner down on top of the art to apply uniform pressure on the image. This keeps all the portions of the image in focus.

▶ **Avoid vibrations and motion.** Avoid jostling the machine while the scan is in progress to keep the light source constant as it passes along the image. If the machine is bumped, you'll see "bumps" in the scan.

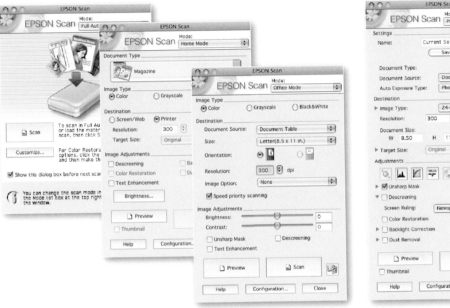

An example of the software that is used with my Epson V300 scanner. Notice how there is a no-brainer "Full Auto Mode," a slightly more detailed "Home Mode," a more robust "Office Mode," and the super-sophisticated "Professional Mode." It's all the same scanner, but the software provides more controls as the user's expertise increases.

Scanner software

You will notice there are very few controls on the scanner itself. All the controls for the scanner are in the software. Each scanner company has its own brand of software. My Epson V300 has four versions of its software depending on the needs of the user (*shown on the previous page*). I always use the Professional Mode.

Setting the resolution

[*Before you read this, I expect that you have already read Chapter 6, so that you understand monitor resolution and printer resolution, LPI and DPI, linescreens and halftones, and all that other resolution stuff.*]

Most scanners let you set the resolution of the scan in one of two ways: by choosing the **actual resolution** for the image, or by choosing the **output media** such as newspaper or magazine.

If you are planning to print on a commercial press, call them up and ask them, "What is the resolution you recommend for my project?" If you are working on an ad for a magazine, call them up and ask them, "What resolution should I use?"

Photograph

Positive Film

Color Negative Film

B&W Negative Film

Illustration

Magazine

Newspaper

Text/Line Art

An example of scanner controls that lists the various types of artwork you need to scan.

Color mode

Some scanning software offers two ways to set the color mode: One uses the digital terminology such as line art, grayscale, RGB, etc. The other uses common descriptions of the type of artwork. Both options can create the proper image, but you still have to know what the terminology means. See Chapter 5 for complete descriptions of each of the color modes.

Scaling during scanning

As discussed in Chapter 6, you should not resize an image unless you understand how it will change the resolution. Fortunately, it's perfectly safe to resize (scale) an image *when you scan it*. For instance, if you have a 4 x 5 image and you need to print it at 8 x 10 at 150 lpi, set the scanner to 300 PPI (twice the linescreen) at 200 percent. The scanning software will do all the math to give you an 8-x-10-inch scanned image at 300 PPI.

Sharpening

Some scanning software lets you apply what's called **sharpening** (also called **unsharp masking**) as you scan. Sharpening compensates for the slight blurring or softness in a scanned image by looking for any differences between the colors of the image. The sharpening command then accentuates these differences, which makes the edges in the image more defined. (Note: Sharpening doesn't *increase* the details in an image; it just makes the details more obvious.)

My scanner software has only four sharpening settings: none, low, medium, and high. This means I have less control over sharpening than I do if I open the scan in Photoshop to apply the sharpening there. That's why I prefer to do my sharpening in Photoshop after I scan an image.

Limit your sharpening to no more than 60–80 percent of the total amount possible. For example, if the software allows you to apply 500 percent sharpening, start with 200 percent; check the scan, then increase the percentage and rescan until the image looks good enough to you. Too much sharpening distorts an image and causes a "glow." If your scanning software does not have a sharpening control, you can sharpen the photo in an image editing program. For an excellent discussion on how sharpening works, see *Real World Scanning and Halftones, Third Edition* by David Blatner, Glenn Fleishman, Steve Roth, and Conrad Chavez.

An example of how unsharp masking improves the appearance of a scanned image. The top left image was scanned using no sharpening. The top right image had a "low" sharpening setting applied. It shows a slight difference. The bottom-left image had a "medium" sharpening setting applied. It shows a bit more details. The bottom-right image had the "high" sharpening setting applied. It has the best appearance.

These images show how much greater control I have when sharpening in Photoshop. The image on the left appears brighter than the highest setting from my scanner. However, the image on the right shows the distortion "glow" that can happen when too much sharpening is applied.

Contrast and color controls

Most scanners have some sort of controls for adjusting the colors and contrast of the image. Most of these controls are also duplicated in programs such as Adobe Photoshop or Corel Paint Shop Pro Photo. As a general rule, adjusting the controls as you scan is better than using other software to adjust the image later.

However, you may find that your image editing software has better controls over color and contrast than your scanner. In that case you will probably want to perform in that program. Experiment with your scanner and see what works best for you.

Scanning printed artwork

In a perfect world, you would always have the original photo-graph, artwork, or negative of the art you want to scan. You would never have only the picture that appeared in last year's annual report because no one can find the envelope with the slides. You would never have only the printed ad from the 1957 issue of a magazine that you want to use in a retrospective of your compa-ny's products. No, you would always have the original artwork and would never need to scan images that have already been printed.

But we don't live in a perfect world, and people do need to scan images that have already been printed. The problem is that when you scan printed artwork, you pick up the original linescreen. (Remember reading about the linescreen in Chapter 6?) Look at the art under a loupe or magnifying glass; if you see dots, that's the linescreen.

You probably won't see any problems in this kind of scan when you view it on the monitor, but you'll see problems when that image is printed: The original linescreen combines with the line-screen for the new scan and causes a moiré pattern (*see page 131 for more information on moiré patterns.*)

There are some steps you can take to avoid moiré patterns when scanning printed artwork, but they're not always effective. If you absolutely must scan printed images, the following pages provide some guidelines for limiting the problems.

Scanning printed line art

There aren't too many problems resulting from scanning line art that's already been printed. All you have to remember is that any gray areas you see aren't really gray—they're actually a pattern of dots. So instead of scanning as grayscale (which will turn the dots into more dots), scan as 1-bit, also known as line art. The solid black areas will appear as solid black and the dots will appear as dots. This shouldn't cause a moiré pattern because you're not "screening a screen"—you're just copying dot for dot.

This image on the left was scanned as **line art at 1200 PPI** directly from a book of old movie ads. Notice how the gray areas are really just a series of dots. Notice also the clean, crisp edges around the solid black areas.

This image on the right was scanned as a **grayscale image at 300 PPI**. Not only are the gray areas fuzzy and muddled, all the solid black areas have blurry edges and there's "noise" in the white areas.

One drawback to scanning printed art that has screens (dots) is that you can't change the size of the scanned image: enlarging causes the linescreen to become more obvious; reducing causes the dots in the linescreen to merge together.

Scanning colored line art

All line art is 1-bit is when it is scanned or created, but all line art does not have to be printed with black ink. Many line art images have been printed with solid colors—perhaps a spot color or 100 percent of a process color—and you can still scan them as line art. The important thing to remember is that the scanner can "see" the color. If the printed line art is a light color like yellow, you need to increase the threshold setting so the scanner can pick up the light color (*see page 70 for an explanation of the threshold for 1-bit images*).

Even though this art is in color, it is actually a single color image with no screens. This art should be scanned as a 1-bit, solid black image. The image can then be recolored in a page layout program.

When you are ready to print this image, remember that you don't have to use black ink; you can print it with any spot color. What is important is that you scan the line art at the resolution of the output device, with a maximum resolution of 1200 PPI (*as explained on page 92*).

This image of Eddie Cantor started out as a grayscale photo, but then was printed as a halftone. I scanned it as line art at 1200 PPI. You can see from the enlargement that the image is simply a series of dots.

Scanning printed grayscale art

Scanning printed grayscale art is actually the same as scanning printed line art in that the gray areas have already been converted to a dot pattern. So all you have to do is capture the original dots by scanning as line art at the resolution of the output device. However, you are under the same constraint as with line art: You can't change the size of the image. Nor can you do any retouching in an image editing program because you will destroy the dot pattern. Try it and you'll quickly see how impossible it is.

Scanning printed color art

Previously printed art in color is probably the hardest type of image to scan and have it look good. If you plan to reprint the scanned image in color, you need to scan as RGB color (not line art), convert to CMYK (unless you plan to print as RGB to an inkjet printer), and then make separations. You must also apply some sort of "descreening" (*see below*) to avoid a moiré pattern. Descreening is not a perfect solution, but it's better than nothing.

Descreening printed art

Most scanning software programs have a control that is supposed to **descreen** printed artwork. In theory this feature will blur or merge the dot pattern into a solid set of pixels—in theory! In practice, descreening is a hit-or-miss affair that avoids a moiré pattern, but softens and distorts artwork so that it's obvious it's not an ordinary image.

Descreening controls are usually listed as the linescreen you are trying to blur: 150 LPI, 133 LPI, 120 LPI, and so on. If you know the original linescreen, choose it; if not, try various settings. The lower the linescreen amount you choose, the higher amount of blur. Keep in mind that descreening doesn't apply to just the dots, but to the entire image; this softens the solid areas of the image as well.

If your scanning software doesn't have a descreening feature, you can try blurring and sharpening the image yourself. Also, if you print to an inkjet printer, that will reduce some of the screening in the image by the very nature of the printing process.

The image on the left was scanned from a printed book. In the middle, the same image was scanned with the descreening command applied. Notice how some of the details are lost. The image on the right was scanned by a professional scanner with all sorts of color corrections, descreening, and other adjustments applied.

Bottom line: Unless you have very expensive equipment, and years of experience, don't expect high-end results when scanning previously printed images. If you need the illustration to look like it was never printed, you should go to a professional scanning service to have them do the scan. At least that's what I would do.

A legal note about scanning

You can't just grab any magazine or book and scan whatever is inside and print it in your own projects. (The same thing applies to just grabbing any old image off of a Web site.) Someone somewhere owns the rights to the image. Most magazines copyright their entire issue. The photographs may be owned by the photographer. Advertisements are copyrighted by the companies that bought the ads. And Web sites are all copyrighted.

You may think "Oh, here in my small town no one will ever see my little printed project." But you never know. A photographer who lives and works far away from you may have a relative living in your own home town who may recognize the image. If you can't get permission to use an image, don't use it.

Scanning projects

Project #1

Sign a blank sheet of paper with various writing implements (markers, roller ball pen, crayons, pencils, fountain pen, etc). Scan the paper as line art. Which signature looks the best? Remember that the next time someone needs their signature inserted into a document.

Project #2

Scan the same sheet from project #1 as a grayscale or color image. Compare the results. Which mode do you think you should use in the future?

Project #3

Scan some photos. Apply various sharpening amounts. Find one that looks good. Remember it.

Project #4

Find an ad in a newspaper or magazine. Scan it. Do you see the linescreen (dots)? Apply the descreening command. Do you think it's good? See, I told you it was hard to get rid of screens.

Project #5

Find a place that does drum scanning in your city. Bring some of the photos you scanned in project #3. Compare the drum scans to the scans you did in project #3. Can you see the difference?

Stock Photos and Clip Art

So maybe you don't have the big budget to hire a world-famous photographer to take pictures for your brochure. Maybe you don't even have the budget to hire a local photographer. Maybe you'd like to put some simple illustrations in your brochure but you can't afford (or can't find) anyone who draws better than your 5-year-old daughter (and she's too busy writing computer programs to help you out).

You don't need to spend a fortune for original art—there are vast collections of professional photos and illustrations made just for you, called stock photography and clip art. Though some professional designers and art directors may turn up their noses at using stock photos or illustrations, there is absolutely nothing wrong with it. In fact, if you know what you're doing, you can get excellent results using these great resources.

History of stock photos and clip art

Stock photos and clip art have been around for many, many years, long before computers.

Stock photos get their name from the days when photographers would sell off their stock of unused pictures to photo agencies who would then resell them. **Clip art** gets its name from the sheets of illustrations and art (mostly black-and-white line art) that were printed in several sizes and sent to designers and ad agencies. These illustrations were cut out (or clipped) from the paper and pasted into position in ads or brochures. Today both photographers and illustrators create artwork specifically for the stock photo and clip art market.

Although stock photos and clip art are nothing new, what is new is how these images are chosen and distributed. In the really old days (maybe 20 years ago) a stock photo company would mail out a huge book of sample photographs for art directors and designers to leaf through. The art director would then choose a photograph, call up the company, have a slide of the image delivered a few days later, and then send that slide out for separations that would be "stripped" into the production film. Whew.

A clip art company would mail out huge sheets (about the

This stock photo from Photospin.com has no identifying marks on the camera or watch. It's a totally generic image.

size of a large newspaper page) of art to subscribers who cut out and pasted the art into mechanicals (layouts on drawing boards).

Today stock photos and clip art are distributed electronically, either on CDs or over the Internet. In fact, if you're working late at night and realize you need a photo, it's possible to find, purchase, and download artwork even at 3 A.M!

How to get them

Stock photos and clip art are available on Web sites. My favorite site for inexpensive photos and illustrations is **iStockphoto.com**. There's also **PhotoSpin.com,** which lets you pay an annual subscription fee and then download as many images as you want with no extra charges. A terrific source for vector clip art is **ClipArt-Lab.com** which sells both collections and individual graphics.

The best thing about these sites is that they have fantastic search engines. You can input a specific image request and get hundreds of options back. So if you are looking for a red pencil on a yellow notepad, you can find it!

You can also buy CDs of clip art or stock photos through computer software catalogs. These CDs usually have some sort of "browser" software that makes it easy to find specific images.

Comp images

Stock photo companies usually let you download a free version of the image at 72 PPI and usually include the company's imprint. These are called **comp images** ("comp" is a traditional designer's term, short for "comprehensive layout"). You can use a comp image in a layout to show a client to see if the client likes the image enough to want to buy it, in which case you'll get the high resolution file, but you're not supposed to use the comp photo in a finished project. You might be tempted to crop out or hide the imprint of the stock photo company—don't do it. It's not only unethical, it's illegal. And besides, at 72 PPI it will look awful if you print it.

These two comp photos, from PhotoSpin.com and iStockphoto.com, both contain the company's imprint.

Stock photo formats

Different stock photo companies provide their images in different file formats (*see Chapter 8 on file formats*). Some companies use TIFF images while others use JPEG at the lowest compression. Whatever the format, there are some things you should look for when purchasing stock photos.

Stock photo resolutions

Many stock photo houses have different prices depending on the pixel dimensions of the image. So you pay less for small images that might only be used on a Web site or screen presentation and more for images that are large enough to print in magazines or advertising.

How many formats are supplied is not as important as what is the largest size supplied. If the largest size is only 5 x 7 inches at 300 PPI, you're not going to be able to use it to cover a full 8½-x-11-inch page.

What color mode?

Almost all high-quality stock photos are RGB images. If you plan to use the photos in a four-color project (CMYK; *Chapter 9*), first use the RGB files to retouch, color correct, combine with other images, and apply special effects. Then convert them into CMYK images for final output.

Selection paths

Stock photos are flattened images. This means that an image on a white background can't be layered on top of another photo or a colored background. That's why I always look for images that include paths.

With a path included in a stock photo, you have a way to select one portion of an image to isolate it from its background. Instead of spending hours tracing around the edge of an image you can select the clipping path in a program such as Adobe Photoshop. You can then use the path to silhouette the image onto a transparent background. This gives you ultimate flexibility in your page layout program.

The stock photo of the New Zealand flag on the left included a path that outlined the flag. I used the path to select the flag and create a transparent background for the middle image. This transparent flag was then added to a new background of the geothermal springs in Rotorua.

Alpha channels

Like selection paths, alpha channels allow you to select one portion of an image to then isolate it or add it to another image. Look for alpha channels as well as selection paths in any stock photos you purchase.

Clip art

The term **clip art** refers to drawings and illustrations rather than photography. These might be cartoons, logos, emblems, symbols, flags, maps, and so on — anything that isn't a photographic image. Just as you can buy professional stock photos, so can you buy professionally drawn clip art.

File formats

There are two types of clip art:

▶ **Clip art in an EPS format** is composed of vector objects (*see Chapter 7 for details and examples*). You can open the art using any vector program, such as CorelDraw or Adobe Illustrator, and modify or alter the artwork in any way you want. This is the most versatile type of clip art because you can easily change colors, move objects around, or combine objects together.

▶ **Art in a TIFF or JPEG format** is a raster illustration (*see Chapter 6*). This type of art is much less versatile. The illustration can be edited only in an image retouching program such as Adobe Photoshop. Look carefully before you purchase this type of clip art to make sure you won't need to edit it.

Complete objects

The quality of clip art depends on how it was created. One thing to look for is that the art is composed of complete objects, which means that all the parts of the illustration are complete, even if they're behind other objects. For instance, you might have an illustration of someone wearing a hat. In your vector drawing program, you might want to remove the hat. If you took the hat off of a complete object, you'd see the top of the head; on an incomplete object, the head would have a big hole in it.

When vector clip art is "complete," it means all of the objects are completely drawn behind others. This is an example of an incomplete object; if you take away the olive and the cheese, you see gaps behind those objects.

Nested groups

Another thing to look for is *intelligent* or *nested groups.* A nested group makes it easy to select an entire element within a drawing. For instance, in the example below, the camera below is composed of dozens of individual objects (*as explained on page 102*). Without nested groups, you have to individually select each of the objects in an element if you want to move or modify it. With nested groups, a single click can select just the one object.

This clip art came with nested groups which made it easy for me to separate the art into individual units. Notice that even the tabs in the book were grouped together. Extra credit: Can you find which elements appear elsewhere in this book? What page? What program might I have used to make the modifications? Can you tell what I did?

Legal stuff

Just because you downloaded an image doesn't mean you have the right to use that image any way you want. There are still some legal things you should keep in mind.

License agreement

You don't actually *buy* the stock photo or clip art—you buy the *license* to use it. There are two types of license agreements: **royalty free** and **rights protected.**

▶ **Royalty free** means that once you have paid for the image or the entire CD of clip art, you can use the images as many times as you like, for as many different layouts, and for as many different products. Watch out, though—some license agreements require an extra fee if you use the image as part of products that are then resold. For instance, you can use an image in a brochure advertising your line of greeting cards, but you can't put the image on the greeting card itself and sell it. Remember, you don't really own the image.

▶ **Rights protected** means you are buying the right to use this image *for a specific project.* You enter into a contract with the stock photo agency and specify exactly how you will be using the image: in a magazine ad, for how many issues, for what area of the country, and so on. This may seem like a hassle, but you get an important benefit in return: The photo or art you use is controlled from being used by a competitor. This means you won't have to worry about seeing your biggest competitor use the exact same photo for their own ad or brochure. (There is a great story about the two political parties in Canada that used the exact same image on their separate brochures. Talk about no differences in Canadian politics!)

Model releases

Any photograph of a "recognizable" person must be accompanied by a model release, a signed form from that person giving their permission to use the photograph in a certain way. For instance, if you have a crowd shot with lots of people who are out of focus, those people are not considered recognizable. But if you have a clear shot of a person looking directly at the camera, that person is recognizable. A good stock photo agency will have signed model releases for all the necessary images. (Some bargain-basement stock photo companies use photographs from foreign countries hoping that the lack of model releases won't affect usage here in the United States.)

However, just because there is a signed release doesn't mean you have a right to use the image in any way you want. You can't use an image in a way that would defame or libel the model. For instance, if you are advertising birth control devices, you had better think twice before you put a stock photo in your brochure—the model in the image may feel you have defamed her if you say she uses your product.

Grabbing stuff from the Web

Some people use the Web as one big free stock photo house. As easy as it is to find images using a Google search, you're not allowed to just grab a file and use it for your own layouts. Seriously! It's the same as when you're scanning images—you're not allowed to steal other's artwork as your own.

So what if you do find an image on a company's Web site that you'd like to use in your brochure? Perhaps you would like to show how that company is doing something good. Look on the Web site for a contact person, usually someone in their public relations office, and ask that person for permission to use the photo in your project. Most likely you will get permission. In fact, they may even send you a high-resolution version of the file.

If you are designing for a non-profit agency, you can also try contacting photographers and artists for samples of their work to use in your projects. Photographers and artists love doing something good—especially if you give them credit in the brochure.

Stock photo and clip art projects

Here are some projects that will help you gain a feel for working with online stock photo and clip art houses. Most of these projects can be completed without spending any money. However, the last two projects do require some cash. So don't worry if you can't finish those projects. They are not required.

Project #1

Visit the following Web sites: iStockphoto.com, Shutterstock.com, PhotoSpin.com, Fotosearch.com, Gettyimages.com, Corbis.com, BigStockPhoto.com, ClipArtLab.com, and 123RF.com. Get a feel for how each site works, and what kinds of art it provides. Look to see if they have free samples. If so, download them.

Don't leave each site till you have gone through the rest of the project assignments.

Project #2

Make up some phrases (such as *red pencil yellow notepad*) and see what results you get from each site. Do some sites have more results than others?

Project #3

Look at the types of artwork available. Notice that there are both photos and illustrations. Does the company offer a way to limit your search to just one?

Project #4

Can you find any of those sites that sell movies and sound files? Would you use those for a print project? What kinds of jobs would you use them for?

Project #5

Download some comp images from the search. Use an image editing program to find their size and resolution. Notice the imprint on the image.

Project #6

Look at the pricing for photos. Does the site charge more for higher-resolution images? Do you think this is right?

Project #7

Look at the pricing for vector illustrations. Does the site have different prices for different sizes of the vector art? Why not? (Answer at the end of this project list.)

Project #8

If you can afford it, purchase one or two photos from one of the sites. Are the photos JPEG or TIFF? If JPEG, is there a lot of compression?

Project #9

If you can afford it, purchase one or two pieces of clip art from one of the sites. What programs do you have that can modify the files? If you can, open the file and see what changes you can make.

Answer to the question in project #7

Vector files are not priced according to size because they are resolution independent (*see Chapter 7*). This means you can scale vector images up as large as you want. So one price fits all.

Answer to the extra credit question on page 195

The art of the camera and the CD-ROM are found on page 158. Both were modified in Adobe Illustrator. The camera was modified by taking out most of the objects that created the image and just leaving a few outlines. The CD-ROM was changed by applying one of the Illustrator brushes to the outside of the circle.

Fonts, Strokes, and Outlines

There's more than just colors and resolutions to consider when working with computer graphics. One important issue is working with fonts. You need to understand how the fonts are installed, what files you need, and how the fonts can be styled and modified.

You also need to understand what happens to strokes, or the outlines around objects, when you reduce or enlarge those objects. You could be in for some nasty surprises if you don't.

Finally, you need to be aware of the technique that converts fonts into artwork. You need to understand when this is a good idea and when it is not.

Font formats

One of the most important things about fonts you need to understand is the three basic font formats, **Type 1**, **TrueType**, and **OpenType**.

Type 1 fonts

Type 1 fonts (also called **PostScript fonts**) are one of the oldest font formats that is still used today. Type 1 fonts come in two separate files:

▶ The file for the **screen font** is used by the computer to display the font.

▶ The file for the **printer font** contains the information that is sent into the printing machine to print the font outlines.

As you can guess from their alternate name, these fonts use PostScript information to draw the font in the printing machine. Many years ago there were some issues with trying to print Type 1 fonts to machines that did not understand the PostScript language. But that's way in the past and nothing you have to worry about.

The most common problem with Type 1 fonts is when the screen font gets separated from the printer font. Without both of those files in the same folder, the font isn't going to work correctly.

Old Wives' Tales About TrueType Fonts

I can't get over how much utter nonsense is floating around about TrueType fonts. The most common myth is that you must never use TrueType fonts for professional output.

There is nothing wrong with using TrueType fonts. They are just as "professional" as Type 1 fonts. They output just fine. This myth gained popularity because of the cheap font collections that some people used to buy off the Web. Those fonts were created by scanning and crudely tracing old type books. But this created clumsy characters that didn't process correctly during printing.

Many print houses got tired of dealing with those cheap fonts. So they issued an edict that banned all TrueType fonts. But what they really were trying to do was stop the use of the cheap TrueType fonts. These days you don't have to worry about using TrueType fonts. The one that came with your computer, or the ones you buy from reputable font houses, are just fine.

TrueType fonts

TrueType fonts were created to combat some of the problems with Type 1 (PostScript) fonts. The major advantage of working with TrueType fonts is that you have only one file to keep track of. This one file contains both the screen font and the printer font.

In addition, there are no issues trying to print TrueType fonts to non-PostScript printers.

All the fonts that are pre-installed on Macintosh machines running OS X are a variation of TrueType fonts called **dfonts**.

OpenType fonts

The newest font format is OpenType. All the fonts that are pre-installed on Windows machines are OpenType fonts.

Like TrueType fonts, OpenType fonts consist of a single file, which makes it easier to keep track of your fonts.

But even better, OpenType fonts can work on either the Windows or Macintosh platform. This avoids a common problem that occurs when files are passed from one platform to another. Without an OpenType font, a file that uses the Helvetica Type 1 font on my Macintosh machine could reflow if I send it to someone who has the Helvetica Type 1 on a Windows machine.

This is because even though the fonts have the same name, they have slightly different settings that could cause the text to move from one line to another.

OpenType fonts come in two different "flavors." The actual font information inside the file can be either PostScript or TrueType. It really doesn't matter much which flavor of OpenType you use. The OpenType fonts that come with Windows machines are Open-Type with TrueType information.

Finally, OpenType fonts can contain many more characters than either TrueType or Type 1 fonts. This means that you can create proper fractions or small capitals quickly and easily.

If you are going to buy fonts to set up your computer, I strongly suggest you invest in OpenType fonts, and not Type 1 or TrueType. (In fact, Adobe only sells OpenType fonts these days.)

Styling fonts

The term "styling fonts" refers to using the automatic italic or bold commands in your software to change a font to its italic or bold versions.

The style controls in QuarkXPress (left) and Microsoft Word (right) that allow you to apply bold and italic styles to fonts.

For instance, you click the letter I in the style controls to convert a font such as Chapparal Pro to *Chapparal Pro Italic*. You click the letter B in the style controls to convert it to **Chapparal Pro Bold**. This is different from the controls in my favorite program, InDe-sign, which requires me to choose the actual style name to apply the italic or bold style of a font. So what's the difference?

Why styling fonts doesn't always work

Let's consider what happens when you click the style control for italic to a font. With a font such as Chapparal Pro, the software (QuarkXPress or Word) changes the font to its italic version. There is no problem to this.

But what happens when you click the style control for italic to a font such as Comic Sans MS, which has a bold version but no italic? In QuarkXPress and Microsoft Word, the typeface gets slanted to the right. This is not an actual italic typeface, however. It is a fake italic! Most professional designers know enough not to use such a fake font. It looks bad. The same thing happens with fonts that don't have a proper bold style. The font just gets thicker in a clumsy way.

How to properly style fonts

Learn which fonts have italic or bold versions. Learn which keystrokes will apply a real bold versus a fake one. Print your document to a PostScript printer or create a PDF to see if the styling is applied correctly.

Small caps styling

There's another type of electronic styling that you should be aware of, applying the small caps style to text. Small caps is a very elegant look where the uppercase letters are large capitals and the lowercase letters are smaller capitals. Programs such as QuarkX-Press and InDesign allow you to apply the electronic style for small caps to text.

Here's where it gets tricky: If the font is the "Pro" version of an OpenType font, the small caps style will substitute the proper small caps version of the characters. If the font isn't an OpenType Pro font, the small caps style converts all the text to capitals and then reduces the size of the lowercase characters. This makes the lowercase capitals look wrong next to the uppercase capitals.

WE GOT ELEGANCE
WE GOT ELEGANCE

The actual small caps (top) looks better than the simulated small caps (bottom). The letter N on the right shows the difference between the electronic small caps and the actual small caps. The gray area shows how the electronic small caps isn't as thick as the proper small caps area in black.

Coloring text

Be careful when applying color to text — especially text smaller than 8 or 9 points. If the color is a single plate, such as cyan, magenta, or yellow, there is no problem. That one plate will look fine. But if the color is a combination of two or more plates, such as a green that is created from cyan, yellow, and black, those three plates may not register correctly when printed. The result is fuzzy letters that can be difficult to read.

Roses are Red. . .Violets are Blue.
Grass is Green. . .And this doesn't rhyme.

This is an exaggeration of why it may be difficult to read colored text at small sizes. Notice how if the color plates don't match up exactly, the text is not clean.

Converting text to outlines

This is one of those situations where you may end up knowing more than the so-called experts at a print shop. I've seen many designers who have been told by their print service providers to select all the text in their document and convert it to outlines.

When you convert text to outlines, you no longer have actual text. The text is changed into *paths* or *outlines* as if they had been drawn using a vector illustration program.

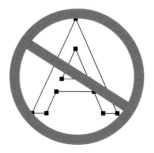

There are several important reasons why you should not do this. First, you lose the ability to edit the text later on. Next, certain effects such as underlines are lost when you convert the text. And finally, you may not realize it, but the text becomes slightly thicker when it is converted to outlines.

The reason for this thick look is the lack of **hinting**. PostScript fonts include hinting specifications that tell the letters how to display within the pixels or dots per inch of the monitor or the printer. When you convert the font from text to paths, you lose the hinting and the font may look thicker on the screen.

The smaller the type, the bigger the problem with thickness; the higher the resolution, the less the problem of thickness. So small type in paths on a laser printer will look worse than the same type on an imagesetter. Type larger than about 9- or 10-point will usually look just fine in paths on any good laser printer and any imagesetter.

So why do so many print shops instruct their customers to convert all the text in their document to outlines? The most common answer is that they are lazy — they don't know how to handle complicated documents and figure that converting the text will cause the file to print more easily. The other answer is more nefarious — they are trying to avoid purchasing the proper fonts to print files.

So what should you do if your print shop tells you to convert all your text to outlines? If you can, find another print shop. You're better off with a shop that doesn't ask for such a bad workflow. Or, if you can't change the print shop, create a PDF of the document. This will avoid any missing font problems. (*For more information on creating PDF files, see Chapter 17.*)

When should you convert type?

There are legitimate reasons why you should convert text into outlines. Most company logos have their text converted to paths so there are no problems with missing fonts. This is especially true for the registered trademark sign (®) that is positioned next to a company logo. The company doesn't want their logo to be listed as having a missing font. So they convert the text into paths.

Another legitimate reason for converting text to paths is to create a special effect. This allows you to manipulate the text as artwork rather than text—you can put pictures inside the letters, distort them, or color them in special ways.

Hairlines

One of the most common problems users create in page layout or vector illustration programs happens when rules (lines) have been set to a **hairline weight**. PostScript code defines a hairline as "the width of one device pixel in the output device." This is "geek speak" that means *the size of the hairline changes depending on the type of printer you output to.*

Hairlines that are visible on the print from a laser printer practically disappear on the output from a high-resolution printer.

Another part of the problem is that not all programs use the same definition of a hairline rule. This means the hairline rules created in a vector illustration program may not match the hairline rules created in a page layout program.

Rather than set a rule width to hairline, it is much better to set it to an absolute measurement: Instead of "hairline," choose ".25 point." Although there may still be some difference in the thickness between a laser printer and a high-resolution output, the .25-point rule won't disappear on the imagesetter output.

Scaling vector lines

As discussed in Chapter 7, one of the advantages of working with vector programs is that the artwork is resolution independent. You can change the size of the art without worrying about pixels clumping together or enlarging. There are no pixels. However, when you make the artwork smaller, you also make the width of the lines (called the **stroke weight**) smaller. For instance, you might import a graphic from a vector program into a page layout program and then reduce the graphic to fit on the page.

When you import illustrations from programs into page layouts, don't scale them down so far that the stroke weight becomes smaller than .25 point. Those lines may not be visible on the final print, or they may not be printable.

The illustration on the left contains both .25 and .125 pt stroke weights. When scaled down on the right, those strokes become almost impossible to see.

If the stroke weight is too small, you need to go back to the original illustration and increase the width of the lines so they can still be seen when reduced. If your artwork is a company logo, you may actually need two versions of your file: a large version of the logo with thin strokes, and a small version with thicker strokes.

Fonts and outlines projects

Here are a few projects which should help you understand working with fonts. Like all the projects in this book, you don't have to finish all of them at once. Rather, they are projects you should continually do as you work.

Project #1

Look at the icons for the fonts on your computer. Are some of the icons different from the others? Some of your fonts may be TrueType and others may be OpenType.

Project #2

Set some text in the regular version of a font. Then set the same text in the italic version of the font. Are the slanted characters in the italic version the same as the regular version? Or does the italic version have letters that are drawn differently?

Project #3

Set some text in a paragraph. Duplicate the paragraph and then convert the text to outlines. Did the spacing between the characters change? How do you feel about that?

Project #4

If you have some OpenType "Pro" fonts on your computer, use a page layout program such as QuarkXPress or InDesign to style the text with proper small caps or fractions. Compare that to Type 1 or TrueType versions of small caps or fractions. Can you see why the OpenType is better?

GETTING YOUR WORK PRINTED AND PUBLISHED

Sending your work off to be printed is a little like sending your child to the first day of school. What should he bring? How should he dress? And does the school have your number in case of emergencies?

With a print job you have to know what kinds of materials the print shop requires. You need to anticipate problems that could develop. And you need a way for them to contact you with questions.

The best-laid schemes o' mice and men
Gang aft a-gley.
ROBERT BURNS

High-Resolution Output

It's difficult in this book, and especially in this chapter, to keep the distinctions clear between all the forms of the word print people use. To **print** can be the action of your desktop printer. "Did you print a copy of the schedule?" **A print** may be the piece of paper that comes out of your desktop printer. "Can I see the print of the menu?" **Print** may also be the reproduction of a job on a press." They'll print the brochures tomorrow." A **printer** can be your desktop machine. "I need ink for the printer." A **printer** is also the person who runs the press. " Ask the printer how much he will charge." **Printing** is the action of making copies from your desktop printer. "Are we printing the schedule in color?" **Printing** is also the professional reproduction process on a press. " They're printing the job next week."

To avoid any confusion, I'll use the word **output** to refer to whatever comes out of any electronic printer, whether it's your inkjet or a high-resolution imagesetter, and **reproduction** to refer to the process of making final copies of the output, whether from a copy machine or a four-color press. I use **print shop** or print service provider for the company that reproduces the work. The **printing machine** is the office printer. And I use the term **print shop owner** for the person who runs the print service provider.

What is a print service provider?

There's more to printing these days than just putting ink on paper. So the term "printer" has been replaced by the broader term **print service provider**. A print service provider (PSP) provides a plethora of services including scanning, image retouching, and color proofs, as well as traditional and digital printing.

One of the more traditional ways a print service provider reproduces your file starts with something called an **imagesetter**. An imagesetter is an extremely sophisticated (and expensive) printer similar, in some ways, to your desktop laser printer. The operator sits at a computer; opens the document; looks through the file to make sure it's okay; chooses "Print" from the File menu; and off goes the document to the imagesetter. The big difference between you and the print service provider is that their imagesetter does not print with toner or color ink cartridges —it outputs separations (*covered in Chapter 9*) onto slick photographic paper or negative film (depending on which one the printing press needs), at extremely high resolutions like 2540 dots per inch. It's really beautiful.

Then you look over that output very carefully and hope there are no problems, typos, surprises, etc. You pay anywhere from $4 to $12 a page for paper output (depending on how many pages you need) and even more for film.

The print service provider uses your slick photographic paper output to make negative film (similar to the negatives you get from your camera), and they use that film to make the plates that go on the printing press.

However, instead of an imagesetter, the more modern print service providers will take your computer file and use it to create a plate directly from the software without any paper or film. This is called **Computer to Plate** or CTP.

Output specifications

When you turn in your files for output, you will need to fill out a form that lists all the details of the job. This is usually called the output specifications, or job sheet. This is so important that I've written a whole chapter on the process; see Chapter 18 for more information on filling out the form.

How to find a print service provider

A Web search for "printers" will send you to a slew of listings for the desktop printing machines. Instead, look for "print service provider." Also ask your favorite local print shop and any designer friends for recommendations of their favorites.

Just make sure you understand the difference between a place that reproduces using copy machines versus one that uses real printing presses.

What to send to the print shop

To output your files, the print service provider needs everything related to that file—all the graphics, the fonts, and of course the file itself. They load all of your files onto their computer. They open your file and print it, not to a desktop printer, but to the high-resolution imagesetter (*see the opposite page*). They need to have the following items:

Native file: This is the page layout file that contains the text and graphics for your project; this is the document you want to output. Programs such as InDesign, Illustrator, QuarkXPress, and CorelDraw can all be used as page layout programs, depending on the project.

Graphic files: Include any scans, illustrations, and clip art you have placed into the page layout. Even though these images are in the layout, the files for the images also need to be sent along. Some programs are fussier than others in this way: For instance, QuarkXPress wants every single little tiny thing you put on any page; PageMaker is much more flexible and will contain the complete information for small images inside the document if you like, rather than make you send dozens of tiny files.

Fonts: You must include each and every font that is used in the document. As we discussed in Chapter 15, even if a print service provider has a font with the same name, it does not mean that it is exactly the same version of the font!

If you use a PC, call the print service provider and make sure they can print from your files. Most print service providers now use PCs as well as Macintoshes, but there are still quite a few who have to open the PC file on a Mac, and the biggest problem that occurs is with fonts. So call first and ask what they recommend.

Applications: You don't have to send the print service provider the application itself—they own the current versions of all the major desktop publishing software packages. But if you use old or obscure software, be sure to call the print service provider and ask if they can output it.

Also notice that I haven't mentioned word processing software—print service providers generally won't output from a word processing application. If you did your entire newsletter in Word-Perfect, that's nice, but the very fact that it's created in a word processing application indicates that the quality of your desktop printer will be enough for the output.

Hard copy: Always include hard copy from your desktop printer. This helps the print service provider know what to expect and will help them recognize problems if something goes wrong. Write notes on the hard copy to indicate colors, special effects you may have used, other things to watch out for, etc.

Package/collect for output

Some programs, such as InDesign and QuarkXPress, make it easy to assemble all the files necessary for output. InDesign calls its feature Package. QuarkXPress calls its feature **Collect for Output**. These commands make a new folder and automatically store a clean *copy* of the document into that folder, along with a *copy* of every file that is necessary for the document to print. The programs even gather up all the fonts and put them in a folder along with the files. You can also get a report that lists all the details of the file, such as the graphics, colors, fonts, etc. While you may not understand everything in the report, your print service provider does and they'll appreciate having the report along with the file.

The disk for the print service provider

Even if you can copy your project onto a USB drive or iPod, most likely, it is a better idea to burn your files onto a CD or DVD.

Label your disk! The print service provider gets hundreds of disks a week, so label every part of it (the case, the disk itself, the envelope it's in, the manila folder, whatever) with your name, phone number, the date, and the name of the job.

Also label your main document and the folder clearly so they can find them easily on their computer; the print service provider needs to find your files to output them, and when they are done they need to throw them away.

Finally, don't copy everything in the folder that contains your job. The print service provider will only get confused by backup copies, alternate layouts, and the previous versions of the project.

Bottom line rule: **Send everything that's necessary to print the job and nothing extra!**

Electronic file transfer

A faster way to send files is to use electronic **file transfer protocol** (FTP). Almost all print service providers have their own FTP site, a special online storage area where you can electronically send your files for output. When they are finished with the job, they send you the output pages by overnight mail. This means you're not limited to working only with the print service providers that might be in your town.

Trapping

Trapping is one of those techniques that you should know about, but most likely should never do yourself. When two colors overlap, one **knocks out** the other. That is, the second color is not really printed on *top* of the first one because that would change its shade. What really happens is the color on the bottom is *removed* from the film so there is just a clear hole, and the second color drops right into that hole.

Now, on the printing press, one color is printed first, and then the other color is printed. Because of the way a press operates, with big rollers going around and paper sliding through very quickly, it's easy for the paper to slide "out of register" just a tiny wee bit. If the second color doesn't drop exactly down into the clear hole made for it, you see a white gap on the final printed product where the white paper shows through.

Trapping is the process that prevents those gaps from appearing. Setting traps is a very intricate and difficult thing for a beginner to do alone. Unless you have the experience, you shouldn't try to set the trap options yourself. It is much better to leave the job to the professionals who have (very) expensive software that does the job automatically. However, although you may not add the trapping yourself, it's important to know what it is and what to do about it. There are techniques you can use while you design your document to avoid the need for trapping at all. *See Chapter 19.*

Imposing your files

As described in Chapter 1, your print shop may ask you to change the order of your pages from **reader spreads** (the order in which your pages will be read), to **printer spreads** (the actual order in which the pages will be reproduced). This is called imposition.

Both InDesign and QuarkXPress have features that will take the files made in reader spreads and convert them into a new document with the correct order of pages on the correct sides of the paper.

These features are great if all you want to do is lay out a simple program to be printed on your desktop printer. **But commercial imposition should really be done only by professionals!** I hear of some print shops who tell inexperienced designers to do the imposition themselves. This is so very wrong!

Why you shouldn't impose yourself

A designer doesn't know enough about the binding method, the thickness of the paper, the number of pages in each signature (*covered in Chapter 1*), to properly impose a document. I consider myself a pretty savvy production person and even I wouldn't trust myself to do that type of work.

If a print shop wants you to impose the pages yourself, try to explain that you're not qualified. Ask them to impose the file for you! Even if you have to pay an extra fee, it is worth the peace of mind that to know that there are professionals in charge of the job.

Sending Acrobat files (PDF) for output

Instead of sending your fragile native files, with all their linked files, fonts, and preferences, it is a much better idea to send Adobe Acrobat PDF files for print work. (PDF stands for **portable document format**.) A PDF file embeds all the fonts and graphics within the file, and it compresses the file so that it's small enough in file size to go through the modem lines quickly. For instance, this chapter, including all the graphics and fonts, is 12.4 MB; the PDF file of this same chapter, including all the graphics and the fonts, is 960 K!

You can make PDF files out of just about any document. Depending on your software, you might go to the File menu and choose something like "Export to PDF," or you might buy the Adobe Acrobat software and make PDFs separately. All desktop publishing software today can make PDFs; check your manual.

Creating a PDF is so important, I'm giving it its own chapter which follows this one.

Sending files for advertising

If you are placing an ad in a newspaper or magazine, you need to send them the material to be inserted into their publication. It is very rare to find a publication that does not accept electronic files. The most commonly accepted file is a PDF document. Some publications accept the native files created by InDesign, QuarkXPress, or other page layout software.

Before you send the publication anything at all—in fact, before you even begin to create the ad—contact their sales or production department and learn their requirements. (*Actually, you remember this from page 5, don't you?*)

High-resolution quiz

Here's a quiz to make sure you understand high-resolution output.

Project #1

Which of the following would you not send along with a job going to the print shop?

A. Fonts; B. Audio files; C. Native files; D. Images

Project #2

Why is it a good idea to send a PDF of your job to the print shop?

A. It contains the fonts; B. It contains the images; C. The layout is frozen in place; D. All of the above

Project #3

Which should you not do to your job unless you have a lot of experience?

A. Impose the file; B. Trap the file; C. A and B; D. None of the above

Project #4

What is the most common file format for advertising sent to publications?

A. Word files; B. Screen shots; C. PDF files; D. None of the above

High-resolution quiz answers

Project #1

Which of the following would you *not* send along with a job going to the print shop?

Answer B: Audio files should not be sent with a design job to a print shop. Those files will only confuse the print shop manager. And besides, it is much too noisy in a print shop to listen to music!

Project #2

Why is it a good idea to send a PDF of your job to the print shop?

Answer D. All of the above: Everything you need to print the document is in the PDF. Plus, the layout is frozen in place so text won't reflow.

Project #3

Which should you not do to your job unless you have a lot of experience?

Answer C. A and B: You're really not qualified to set the traps nor impose the pages into signatures. This type of work is best left to the professionals.

Project #4

What is the most common file format for advertising sent to publications?

Answer C. PDF files: It is very rare for a publication to ask for anything except a PDF file.

Acrobat and PDF Files

Creating a PDF document is similar to packing for a trip. When I go on a trip I put everything I need — clothes, shoes, toiletries, computer cables — neatly into a suitcase. I may use a list to make sure I haven't forgotten anything. I put a tag on the bag in case it gets lost in transit. Finally I zip up all the compartments to make sure no one opens the bag and that nothing falls out.

The process is similar when you create a PDF file that you want to send to a print service provider. (PDF stands for portable document format.) When you create a PDF document, you have packed all the pages, layout, images, and even fonts into the PDF suitcase (wrapper) that holds all the information needed to print the document. There's even some compression (like those roll-up travel vacuum bags) that makes sure everything takes up the smallest possible space.

Glossary of Acrobat terms

There are so many different terms associated with Acrobat and PDF documents. This little glossary will help you sort them out.

Acrobat: The software sold by Adobe Systems that allows you to open, edit, and save PDF documents.

Acrobat Distiller: The software module, sold as part of the Acrobat bundle, that creates PDF files. This is the actual software that is used when the Adobe PDF printer driver is chosen to create a PDF file. (See the section on creating PDF files, in this chapter.)

Adobe PDF printer: The printer driver that appears when the Acrobat software is installed. Choosing this option lets you create a PDF using Acrobat Distiller in the background.

Adobe Reader: The free software that allows you to open and view PDF documents. Depending on how the original PDF was saved, you may be able to fill in forms and/or add comments using Adobe Reader (also called Reader). This application was originally called Acrobat Reader but the name was changed to avoid confusion with the commercial product.

PDF: The file format of documents created by Acrobat and other software. The PDF file format is now an internationally recognized file format standard and can be created by both Adobe and non-Adobe software.

A little background

First released in 1993, Acrobat and PDF documents didn't really gain wide acceptance as a file format for print service providers until around 1999. That's when a robust set of print production features was added to the PDF document format.

Suddenly print service providers had a way to print a document without worrying about missing elements or text reflowing. Instead of asking for the native application files, they began asking for PDF documents. And the rest is the success of PDF.

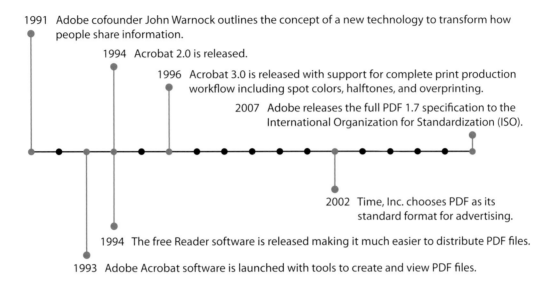

1991 Adobe cofounder John Warnock outlines the concept of a new technology to transform how people share information.

1994 Acrobat 2.0 is released.

1996 Acrobat 3.0 is released with support for complete print production workflow including spot colors, halftones, and overprinting.

2007 Adobe releases the full PDF 1.7 specification to the International Organization for Standardization (ISO).

2002 Time, Inc. chooses PDF as its standard format for advertising.

1994 The free Reader software is released making it much easier to distribute PDF files.

1993 Adobe Acrobat software is launched with tools to create and view PDF files.

A timeline of some of the important events in the development of Adobe Acrobat and the PDF file format.

Benefits of creating PDF files

There were three primary reasons why PDF became so popular with designers and print service providers.

All-in-one portability

Perhaps the most important reason people use PDF documents is that they take all the elements needed to print a document and compact them into a single file. All the images, fonts, color information, and page information necessary to print the file are all contained in the single PDF file. In addition, you can send a PDF to anyone and they can open it with the free Adobe Reader software. You don't have to worry that they might not have the same layout program that you used to create the file.

Compressing files

Another reason why PDF files are popular is the file compression that is applied. A PDF file is smaller than all the individual elements added together.

Troubleshooting problems

The very act of creating a PDF is a form of printing. Therefore, if there is a problem that might cause a file to fail to print, you will most likely see it when you try to create the PDF. This becomes an important troubleshooting guide.

However, the opposite is also true. If you can convert your file into the PDF format, most likely it will output correctly at the print service provider. PDF files will also print slightly faster than native files because part of the print processing has already been done.

Ways to create PDF files

As the PDF file format has become more popular, there have been many more ways to create PDF documents. Some are from Adobe; others are from third-party software companies. One important thing to remember, though: Not all PDF documents are created the same. Your print service provider may not want you to create a PDF using certain techniques.

Using Distiller

Over the years, creating PDF files has gotten simpler and simpler. Originally we had to create a PostScript file, then take that file and send it to the Acrobat Distiller software. Distiller would then create the PDF document according to its settings.

You young'uns have it much easier. As long as you have installed the Adobe Acrobat software, all you have to do is choose Print from the menu for your software. You can then pick the Adobe

PDF driver from the print dialog box. You use that dialog box to select all the proper options. And then click the Print button.

As you go back to work, or read your email, or feed the cat, Acrobat Distiller works with the printer driver to create the PDF file.

Using applications

If you work with programs such as InDesign, QuarkXPress, Illustrator, Photoshop, or other professional layout and illustration programs, you will find the options to create PDF files by choosing Export or Save As. These commands don't use Distiller to create the PDF file.

For the most part you should use the Export or Save As commands from the native software. Unless you have found some esoteric reason, the PDF documents created by exporting are just fine. (*See the sidebar below for a comment on this process.*)

Using the Mac operating system

If you use a Macintosh running OS X, you may have found the Print dialog box command to Save as PDF. If you've tried it, you'll agree it's pretty amazing. No extra steps, no settings, and definitely no waiting around for Distiller to launch and do its thing.

The Distiller Versus Export Debate

There is a debate between some print service providers who insist that their customers *only* use Distiller to create PDF files and people like me who create their PDF files using the Export commands in InDesign or QuarkXPress. In trying to understand their reasons for insisting on Distiller, my best guess is that they do it because they've always worked that way.

They also may have tried to process a PDF created using the Export command and didn't understand how to set the Export options to match the output from Distiller. This is especially true when using InDesign, which can create more advanced PDF files than those from Distiller.

Don't get scared by those who tell you the Export command isn't a good way to create PDF files. As long as you know what you are doing, using this command should not cause any problems.

However, if you run into an old-timer who refuses to accept anything except Distiller-created PDF documents, go along with them if they are the only place that will do your job. Life is too short to argue about how to make PDF files!

So what's with the command? Why doesn't everyone just use the Macintosh Save as PDF command? Why bother with buying Acrobat and Distiller? Why wade through all the steps in InDesign or QuarkXPress?

The reason is that as handy as that command is, it was never intended to create professional, production-ready PDF documents. It was added to OS X to give Macintosh users a quick and free way to send copies of their documents to friends who might not have the same Macintosh software (i.e, Windows users).

But the way the Mac operating system creates the PDF may not be up to the latest PDF specifications. (*Remember the timeline on page 223? The specifications that were certified by the ISO — the International Organization for Standardization?*) This won't cause any problems when you want to send a Holiday PDF to everyone in your family. But it could cause a print service provider to reject your file.

Using third-party software

So why doesn't everyone just buy Adobe products and make PDF files using Distiller or the built-in PDF commands? Two reasons: First, not everyone can afford Distiller. Second, companies such as Quark Inc. may not want to pay Adobe for the license to use the Acrobat electronic controls to make PDF documents.

So there are many third-party (non-Adobe) products that let you create PDF files. Some are quite professional, such as the **Global Graphics' Jaws PDF Creator**. This product was based on the technology used in the Harlequin RIP, software that prepress veterans recognize as an all-time classic for reliability and fidelity. (This is the underlying software used by QuarkXPress when it creates PDF files.) Another is the **Nuance PDF Converter**, which offers a tool bar that can be used with Microsoft Word.

However, there are also many freebie, ad-driven, or cheap PDF-creation products out there. (I won't mention their names — they don't need any publicity from me.) These products may or may not do a good job in creating production-ready PDF documents.

The only way to tell if a non-Adobe PDF application is worth using is to try it yourself. If you get good results, congratulations. If not, well, don't say I didn't warn you.

Setting the PDF controls for print

You may feel a little overwhelmed when you first look at the controls for creating PDF files. There are literally hundreds of different combinations. However, once you understand what those controls do, you'll see it's not really that complicated. And fortunately, almost all the different programs that create PDF files use the same sets of controls.

Using the presets

If you're lucky, you can use one of the presets that ships with Acrobat or other applications that create PDF documents. Adobe has provided settings such as **Press Quality** or **High Quality Print**. Both of these presets automatically adjust all the other controls to the proper settings for professional print output.

Adobe has also included a group of presets with the label **PDF/X**. PDF/X is a collection of settings that various magazines, newspapers, and print shops have agreed on as a standard for print publishing. If you get a request for one of the PDF/X presets, you just choose it and export or create your PDF file. You don't have to worry about the specific settings.

General

The General settings are the options for the entire document. It's where you can specify the pages you want and what things should be included in the document. It's very easy to remember what should be included in a PDF for print publishing: **Don't include anything extra!**

Thumbnails, tags, layers, and interactive elements (covered later in this chapter) are only going to cause your print provider to get upset and could possibly keep the job from printing properly.

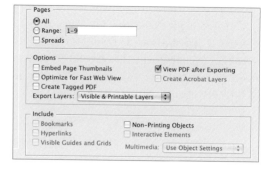

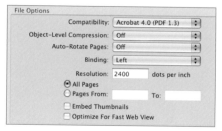

The general settings from InDesign (left) and Distiller (right).

Compression

The options for compression may appear daunting at first. But here's a general idea of what they do. (Trust me, I'm only covering the very basics in this chapter. A full discussion would take an entire book.)

The point of compression is to make the PDF file size smaller than it would be if you just shipped the layout, the images, and the fonts together in a folder. The place where compression does the most work is in the size of the images.

You can set the compression options individually for color, grayscale, and monochrome (1-bit) images. (*See Chapter 5 for descriptions of each of these types of images.*) The reason for this is that some people need better quality in their color images than they do for the others. Having three settings of compression options gives you flexibility in how the various images are handled.

The Sampling menu from Distiller.

In order to understand the compression options, you need to look at the **Downsampling and Subsampling controls**. The first thing to understand is that sampling means throwing away pixels. There are three different ways those pixels are thrown away. **Bicubic Downsampling** is the most sophisticated, but takes more time. **Average Downsampling** is a little faster but not as smooth. **Sub-sampling** is the fastest, but creates the roughest results.

The Sampling menu with the resolution settings for downsampling.

The next thing to understand are the settings for what pixels should be thrown away. Let's say you've taken a photo that is 3872 pixels wide and 2592 pixels tall. (*I covered pixels way back in Chapter 6.*) If you scale that image down to an **effective resolution** of 300 pixels per inch (PPI), the image's dimensions are about 13 inches by 8 ½ inches. But if you scale the image down further, to about 6 inches by 4 inches, the effective resolution goes up to 645 PPI.

Now, that higher resolution isn't going to hurt the document or the image or the printing process. But it is going to add to the file size of the PDF document. That's when it makes sense to apply some downsampling. The numbers in the sampling options are you telling Acrobat, "If an image is over a certain number of pixels per inch, please throw away those extra pixels so that the resolution of the image is a lower amount." For most professional printing, these settings consist of the following rule: **For images over 450 PPI, lower the resolution to 300 PPI.**

The final setting is the actual compression that will be applied to the image. This is different from throwing away pixels. It is applying electronic changes to the actual image to make the file smaller. There are several different types of compression. The most common is **JPEG compression**. This is the compression that creates the blocky images you may have seen on Web pages (*and which I illustrated back on in Chapter 8*).

The **Automatic (JPEG)** setting is used for color and grayscale images and automatically applies the best quality for the type of image. If you're going to apply compression, this is the easiest way to apply it. The JPEG setting uses the specific image quality that has been chosen. Both of the JPEG compression settings are **lossy**. This means they will result in some loss of the original image data. That is when you need to choose how much of the original image is retained. Choosing a lower quality results in an image that looks less perfect. However, a lower quality image creates a smaller file. The ZIP compression option can be lossy or **lossless** (no information lost). When you work with images that have large solid areas of color, such as charts and graphs, choose ZIP compression.

The Compression menu (left) and Image Quality menu (right).

Things are a little different with monochrome or bitmapped images. First, the amount of resolution is much higher. This is because monochrome (1-bit) images are output at a minimum of 1200 PPI. So you throw away pixels (subsample) only when the resolution is above 1800 PPI.

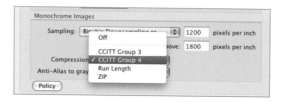

The monochrome Compression menu.

Also, the compression options are different. The **CCITT Group 3 option** is best for fax images. The **CCITT Group 4** setting is the all-purpose setting for print output. **Run Length** is the best setting for images that contain large areas of solid black or white.

So what's the best setting for print? That's easy. Just choose one of the PDF/X presets and you're good to go. Of course, if your print provider wants other settings, you should always use those options.

Marks and Bleeds

As covered in Chapter 18, professional print output will often apply special marks and information around the print area of a file. You may also need to set a bleed for artwork that touches the trim. (*See Chapter 4 for an explanation of the a bleed amount.*) These settings are controlled using the options in the **Marks and Bleeds** category of the Save As PDF dialog box.

You should consult with your print provider as to which marks and bleed settings they require. This is one of those areas where the presets for PDF/X won't help you as they don't set any marks and bleeds.

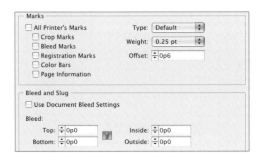

The Marks and Bleed and Slug options in InDesign.

Fonts

In most cases the fonts are automatically embedded in the PDF. Some font designers set an option in their font that prevents it from being embedded. If you use this type of font, tell your your print service provider. As long as they have the font loaded on their computer, they can output your file with no problems.

One of the terms that confuses people is the concept of **subsetting** fonts. As I mentioned earlier, one of the reasons people use PDF documents is that the font is packaged inside the document. Most likely, you have not used every character contained in the font. For instance, I doubt that you would use the characters for the Japanese yen (¥), a pilcrow (¶), and a double dagger (‡) all in one document.

So do you want to include all the characters in the font, which would add to the file size, or do you want to include just the actual characters that you have used? The actual characters you have used is called the subset of the font.

The setting for subsetting fonts in a PDF from InDesign.

When the subset field is set for 100% it means you'd have to use every single character in the font in order to have the entire font embedded in the PDF. Since it's unlikely you've used every single character in the font, the PDF will embed just those characters you've used — the subset. This keeps the file size small. If the subset field is set to 0%, you are forcing the PDF to include all the characters in the font. This will make the file size larger.

Why would you want to include every character in the font? Let's say you subset your fonts, and later need your output provider to edit the PDF. Perhaps they need to change a price from dollars to yen. If you haven't used the yen sign elsewhere in the document, they won't be able to make the edit unless they have the font installed on their system.

Other

Most of the other settings for PDF files are far too advanced to go into in this book. However, the best way to apply those options is to ask your print service provider what they require. If you are working all by yourself, choose one of the PDF/X settings or the preset for **Press Quality Output**. That will give you a setting that shouldn't mess up your file.

Security

One thing that you should *not* set are any security options. The security options allow you to lock a file to keep someone else from opening it or making changes. Don't do it! You're only going to make your print provider very angry when they have to unlock those settings.

Non-printable PDF elements

There are many other features and attributes that are possible to include in PDF files. Most of them are not used in professional print production. The following are elements that you *shouldn't include* in a PDF that will be output by a print service provider:

- ▶ Hyperlinks
- ▶ Movies
- ▶ Sounds
- ▶ Annotations
- ▶ Layers
- ▶ Tags
- ▶ Bookmarks
- ▶ Thumbnails
- ▶ Layers
- ▶ Comments

Output Specifications

When you go to a print service provider's Web site or visit them in person, they give you a job form to fill out. If you have never done it before, filling out this form can be intimidating because there are all sorts of strange terms you may not understand. Fortunately, if you've read this far in this book, you should be somewhat familiar with the terms.

But since I can't be with you all the time, let's fill out a sample form to see what the various topics are all about !

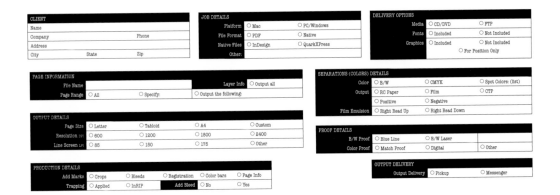

Filling out the form

Completing an output specifications form doesn't have to be a frightening experience. All you're doing is asking them to print your electronic files in a certain way.

The form is usually divided into two types of information: information about you and information about the job. You should know the information about you, so you've already got some of the form filled out!

Although each print service provider has its own particular set of specifications, the following form is fairly standard and should help you understand what is being requested.

Not all print providers will ask for all the following items. Similarly, some print providers may ask for other information. Just remember, you won't look stupid if you don't know the answer to a certain item.

Ask questions! Print providers love it when designers ask them questions. It lets them know that you're willing to work to make sure your job prints correctly.

CLIENT		
Name		
Company		Phone
Address		
City	State	Zip

Client information

Who's the client? This simple question is tricky: You may be working for someone you call *your* client, but as far as the print service provider is concerned, you are *their* client. So the client information the form is asking for is *your* name, company, address, etc. Some shops may ask for an office phone number and a cell number because they will most likely be working on your job overnight. So if there are any problems with the file, they would like to be able to contact you after you've left your office.

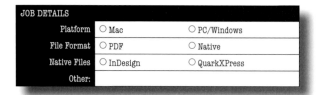

JOB DETAILS		
Platform	○ Mac	○ PC/Windows
File Format	○ PDF	○ Native
Native Files	○ InDesign	○ QuarkXPress
Other:		

Job details

This is simple: The print service provider needs to know what type of files you're sending them. They want to know the platform that created the file (important for working with fonts), what type of file (native or pdf), and if it's a native file, what program you used.

The print service provider will also want to know what programs, including version numbers, you used to create the graphics in the file in case there are any problems that require them to open those files.

I've seen instructions from one place where they flat out refuse to take anything but the very latest versions of the page layout software. This is astonishing because most designers complain that their print service provider won't take files from the latest application because they haven't gotten around to upgrading their software. These are two reasons why you should just send pdf files!

Be aware that some providers won't take certain programs. For instance, Microsoft Publisher isn't accepted by many shops. In those cases, you should submit a pdf of your job.

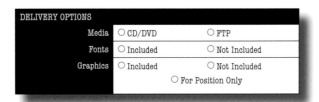

Delivery options

The shop may want to know how the file is coming into their office. For instance, they don't want to be looking for a CD-ROM disk if you've sent the file electronically.

They also need to know if you've supplied fonts to go with a native file. If you have, someone will have to load those fonts into their system. Read the license that came with the fonts. If permitted, you can send the fonts along with the file. If not, you'll need to alert the service provider that you're using those fonts.

Finally, they may want to know if you've sent the graphics separately from the file itself or have embedded them so that they are part of the pdf or native file.

Some shops may ask if your graphics are **FPO** (**For Position Only**). What this means is that you have placed low-resolution versions of the scanned images. The print service provider has the high-resolution versions, which they will swap for your FPO placeholders. This is a somewhat outdated workflow, but may still be used by some catalog publishers.

PAGE INFORMATION				
File Name			Layer Info	○ Output all
Page Range	○ All	○ Specify:		○ Output the following:

Page information

It may seem obvious to you which file you want output, but you might have a page layout file, graphics, illustrations, fonts, and other files in the same folder, and the service bureau has no clue exactly which file (or files) you want output. Write down the exact name of the file. If you need several files output, you should fill out a separate form for each individual file.

The page range is more interesting. If you have a document with several pages, you might not want all those pages to be output. My own opinion is not to send extra pages along with the job. It's only going to slow down the production people to have to specify exactly which pages you want. Delete the pages you don't need.

Similarly, if you have certain layers that you don't want to print, you should delete those layers before you send the job to be output. I wish I could send a multi-layered document to the print shop and have them simply turn on and off the layers I want to hide or show. But I can't trust the operators to follow my instructions exactly. It is much safer to create multiple versions of a file with just the layers you want to be output.

OUTPUT DETAILS				
Page Size	○ Letter	○ Tabloid	○ A4	○ Custom
Resolution DPI	○ 600	○ 1200	○ 1800	○ 2400
Line Screen LPI	○ 85	○ 150	○ 175	○ Other

Output details

This is where you start specifying your job. The size of the page is obvious. Remember, this is the size of the trim.

Resolution (DPI) and linescreen (LPI)

You should remember our discussion of **resolution (DPI)** as well as the **linescreen (LPI)** back in Chapter 6. Be aware that there are many different linescreen values. But not all linescreens are available for some resolutions. Check with your print service provider if you are uncertain about filling in these values.

SEPARATIONS (COLORS) DETAILS			
Color	○ B/W	○ CMYK	○ Spot Colors: (list)
Output	○ RC Paper	○ Film	○ CTP
	○ Positive	○ Negative	
Film Emulsion	○ Right Read Up	○ Right Read Down	

Separations (colors) details

This is where you specify the number and type of colors in your document.

Color

B/W stands for a black-and-white or a one-color job. CMYK is a four-color job. If you have spot colors, you need to indicate them as well as list which colors you expect to see on a separate spot color plate.

Output

The **output medium** is the material you want the print service provider to give you as output. For instance, you might want your job output onto special paper if you are taking it somewhere else for reproduction.

RC paper: RC stands for *resin coated*. RC paper is similar to photographic paper. It gives the most consistent black images and crisp edges. It's beautiful. Many local magazines and newspapers accept black-and-white ads on RC paper.

Film output: Film looks like a sheet of clear acetate. Full-color jobs are almost always output to film. Each color has its own separate piece of film, so a four-color job (cmyk) prints four pieces of film per page; these are the separations. Not many print providers use film. (Seeing it on an order form may just be a leftover from years ago.) If you choose film, you may have to specify whether you want it positive or negative, and whether the emulsion should be up or down (*see below*).

CTP: CTP stands for **computer-to-plate**. This process skips creating RC paper or film and goes directly to making a plate. (This is also called direct-to-plate.)

Positive or negative

Film is basically transparent until it is exposed. Most film output is exposed as a **negative** image—the white areas of your document are black in the negative film; the black areas of the document are clear. The print shop needs negatives because of the way plates are made for the press. You might find a print shop that requests positive film, but it's rare.

Emulsion up or down

The **emulsion** is the surface of the film that contains the chemicals that react to create the image. Because film is basically transparent and can be viewed from either side, the emulsion is the only way to tell which is the "front." The emulsion is the dull side; the other side of the film is shiny. Ask your print provider which one they prefer.

Production details

The term **printer's marks** describes many different types of marks and bits of information that are printed outside the "live" image area. This means the marks will show up on the oversized film or paper output, but they are located outside the "live" area that will be seen in the finished product. The most common of these marks are crop marks and registration marks.

Crop marks

The print service provider does not output your job onto 8½-x-11-inch pieces of paper. They output your pages onto rolls of paper or film that are much bigger than the final size of your project. Because the output is bigger than your document, you can't tell where the edges are anymore. So we put crop marks at the corners.

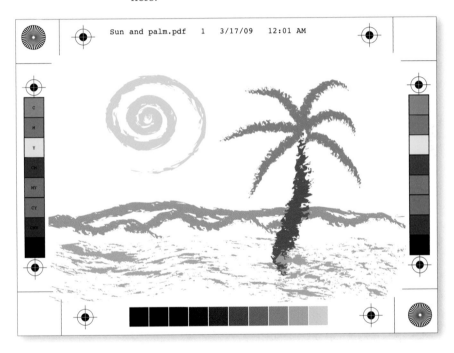

A page with crop marks, registration marks, color bars, and page information. Notice how late it was when I created this art.

It's unnecessary to draw the crop marks in yourself if the page size of your document is the size of the trim; that is, if your final designed document is 5x7 inches and you made a 5x7 inches document in your page layout software, then crop marks will automatically be added where they belong. You simply tell the service bureau that you want them and they shall appear. But if your designed document is 5x7 inches and the layout page is

8½-x-11-inches, the crop marks will appear at the corners of the 8½-x-11-inch size, not the 5x7 inches size! You'll have to add the 5x7 inch crop marks by hand. This is why it is important to create the size of the page as the final trim size.

Registration marks

Registration is the process of aligning each of the separate pieces of film for color projects. The marks look like crosshairs in a rifle scope (*shown on the previous page*). All four pieces of film are laid over each other, and small pins are placed through the center of the marks to ensure that all the pieces line up correctly and exactly. Some software lets you define registration marks as centered or not centered between the crop marks. Your print shop can tell you which setting they prefer.

Color bars

Color bars are rectangles of different percentages of the different colors. They are used when the job is on the press to judge the correct percentages of the colors in the file.

Page information

The page information adds a line of text with information such as the name of the file and when it was printed. In the case of a PDF, the information shows when the document was created. Without the page information, it would be difficult to tell what the little bits of film are for.

Trapping

On the off chance that you have applied your own trapping to the document, this setting lets you specify that the traps have already been applied. The alternative to doing the traps yourself is to let the print service provider apply the trapping as part of the print processing. This is called **inRIP** trapping.

I hope I made it very clear in Chapter 16: **You really shouldn't try to apply trapping yourself**. Really!

Add bleed

Way back in Chapter 4, I covered why you set a bleed area around a document. This setting in the output form simply instructs the

---

The Book Cover

Did you notice the cover of this book is a simulation of the proof of a document? There are crop marks, color bars, registration marks, bleed marks, and page information. It's the perfect cover for this book!

print service provider if you forgot to set the bleed and would like them to do it for you.

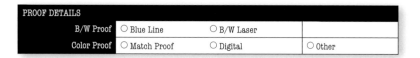

Proof details

You may request some sort of color proof along with your output. The different types of proofs are described in detail in Chapter 20.

Delivery details

This is simple: The print service provider needs to know if you're going to come and pick up the job or if you want it sent to you. If you need it sent, they need your address; if you're going to come pick it up, they'll hold it for you. You can also ask them to call you when the job is complete.

Output project

Create a simple layout and take it to a print service provider. Fill out their output form. Do you understand everything? If not, ask questions.

Trapping

Trapping is a little like buying a boat. The saying about buying a boat is, "If you have to ask the price, then you can't afford it." My feeling about trapping is, "If you have to ask what it is, then you shouldn't do it."

In fact, as I am writing this chapter I can hear production managers all over the country yelling ,"No, no! Don't write about trapping. Your readers shouldn't get involved with trapping! It'll only confuse them."

I wish I could skip talking about trapping, but the fact is that someone, somewhere, is going to mention trapping to you and it will be much better if you have some understanding of what it's all about.

Keep in mind that this is hardly a detailed lesson on trapping — these are just the basic facts with a couple of suggestions for how to avoid the need for it.

What is it and why do it?

Before you understand how to trap, you need to understand *why* to trap. Think about some of those rather horrible inserts you get in Sunday newspapers—the ones with all those coupons for products you never buy. Have you ever seen one of those pages where everything is slightly off-kilter, where colors don't fit neatly inside the spaces where they belong, where objects look like they are out of position? We say the colors are **out of registration**, often called **misregistration**.

Misregistration occurs for various reasons: The paper on the printing press shifts, the plates move, a meteor hits the building (just kidding). But the result is that one of the colored inks is printed just a wee bit out of place. This causes a gap between the colors where the white paper shows through.

Misregistration can't be prevented. There are some presses that are less likely to have registration problems, but you won't find any printing press that prints in perfect registration all the time. So we need to compensate for the inevitable misregistration. That's where trapping comes in.

Color knockouts

Let's say you put one object filled with one color over another object filled with a different color. What happens in the area where the two objects overlap? When you make the separations for your file, the top object knocks a hole in the bottom object. The hole is called a **knockout**. When the two color plates are registered correctly, the top object sits perfectly inside the knockout. When the two color plates are misregistered, the top object is slightly off from the knockout, creating the slight gap. If the paper is white, you see a white gap.

Trapping the color

The nasty gap occurs because the top object is exactly the same size as the knockout. If the knockout was slightly smaller or the object slightly bigger, there would be an area where the two colors would **overlap**. Then if one object moved slightly, there still wouldn't be a gap. The **overlap is the trap**, and you can see it in printed pieces where the overlap of the two adjacent colors creates a third color.

Avoiding the need for trapping

Worrying about trapping is a little like worrying about being struck by lightning: Yes, some people do have problems with the registration of colors, and some people do get struck by lightning, but most people never have to worry about it.

Most printing presses today have much less trouble with misregistration than they used to. As long as you understand some of the principles of trapping, you may never have to trap at all (and as long as you stay indoors during a lightning storm, you may never get hit by lightning). Following are some of the ways to avoid trapping problems.

Keep colors apart

This is so basic that many people forget it. If you want to avoid registration problems, just don't let your colors touch. For instance, if you have red type over a blue background, you might be afraid of a misregistration. If you add a white outline around the type, you have created a "buffer zone" where the two colors won't touch. As long as the colors don't touch, you don't have to worry about misregistration. And as long as you don't have to worry about misregistration, you don't have to create traps to avoid noticeable gaps.

Milk carton and soft drink cup designs are excellent examples of physically separating colors to avoid trapping. These items are printed on presses that have the potential for enormous misregistration. The size of the traps necessary to avoid gaps would be huge and very noticeable. So most designers avoid the need for trapping by adding white around the elements. No matter how badly the colors are registered, there is no need for traps because the colors don't touch.

Use an overprint

The easiest way to avoid misregistration is to **overprint** colors. Overprinting prevents the knockout in the color underneath so the top color just prints directly on top of the other color. Without the knockout there is no way the nasty gaps can appear. All vector illustration and page layout programs let you overprint selected objects and colors.

Of course, when you overprint you have to accept the fact that your colors are going to change. For instance, yellow overprinting blue creates green. That's not so bad if you *want* to create green, but you will have a slight problem if only half of the yellow object overprints blue: Half of the yellow object will be green, and the other half will still be yellow.

If you have software that allows you to turn on a preview of overprinting, you can see what the effect is. If not, you need to print your file with the Simulate Overprint setting turned on in the printer dialog box. However, you shouldn't turn on overprinting willy-nilly. You could wind up with a muddy effect for your colors.

If you are unsure of what you are doing when you apply overprinting, talk to the print provider that will be printing your job; they will give you the best advice.

Use common plates

Trapping is less of an issue in four-color process printing (*see Chapter 9 for more information on process colors*) than it is in spot color printing. (Milk cartons and drink cups are usually printed with spot colors.) Remember, the goal of trapping is to avoid the gap between colors where the paper shows through.

When two colors share a common plate (or several plates), the misregistration from one color butting up against another color isn't as noticeable. For instance if there is a little magenta in a blue background, and a little cyan in a red object, there isn't any need for trapping.

If the misregistration occurs, the art still won't fit exactly into their knockouts. But instead of a white gap, there will be a gap filled with either a light tint of magenta or cyan. That tint of color is less objectionable than the glaring white.

Should *you* trap?

So let's say after all this you decide you want to set the traps in your software (alarm bells should be going off in your head). After all, most software has built-in trapping commands. You'll just open the dialog box, set a few numbers, and be finished, right? Not really! Setting the size of traps is a very precise science. You need to know the type of printing press, the type of paper, the inks, and many other technical issues before you can decide how big the traps should be. Your print provider has knowledge built on long experience.

But let's say you do have an idea of how much to trap. Should you do it then? No. Especially not if you are combining text in your page layout program with photos or vector illustrations. The page layout program can only set the traps for the elements that were created in that page layout program — it can't trap graphics that were brought in from another application. So if you build traps for a headline in InDesign or QuarkXPress, the trap won't do anything when that headline prints on top of an illustration brought in from Illustrator.

The best solution is: Let the print service provider set the traps! They have special software dedicated to trapping all the elements on your page together. **Dedicated trapping software is the best choice for trapping and the people at the print provider are the best people to run it.** (In case you were wondering, trapping software costs thousands of dollars. It's not meant for poor creatures like us to use. Thank goodness.)

Trapping quiz

Project #1

You have a blue circle at the top left of your page and a yellow circle on the bottom right. Do you need to set the traps?

Project #2

You have black text set to overprint onto yellow. Do you need to set the traps?

Project #3

You have green text (c: 100, m: 0, y: 100, k: 0) sitting on a blue (c: 100, m: 20, y: 0, k: 0) background. Do you need to set the traps?

Project #4

You have a 1-color job that has vector art in it. Do you need to set the traps?

Project #5

The final output of your job is the desktop printer. Do you need to set the traps?

Project #6

You want to buy a boat but need to know the price. Should you buy it?

Project #7

A friend suggests that you set the traps for your layout before you send it to the print provider. Should you set the traps?

Trapping quiz answers

The quick answer to all the projects is, "No!" The explanations below tell you why.

Project #1

Since the two colors don't touch there is no need to trap.

Project #2

If one color overprints another, there is no need to trap.

Project #3

The common cyan plate makes it unnecessary to trap.

Project #4

Vector or raster art in a job doesn't matter. As long as it's a single-color job there is no need to trap.

Project #5

There are no separations when you send the job to a desktop printer. So there is no need to trap.

Project #6

If you have to ask the price, you shouldn't buy it.

Project #7

No. Trapping is a technique better left to the professionals.

Preflight and Proofing

Waiting until you have 20,000 finished copies of your project is a little late to find out the headline is misspelled. Or the text can't be read at that point size. Or the color of the product is wrong.

The term "preflight" was coined by Chuck Weger back in 1990 at the Color Connections conference in San Francisco. The term came from the list of actions that airplane pilots take to ensure their plane is ready for flight and to make sure the plane doesn't crash.

Chuck used it to signify that the file was ready for output and it wouldn't crash the print processor. The term preflight soon became an industry standard used by many applications. (And no, Chuck doesn't get royalties on it.)

A proof is a single-copy prototype of the finished product that helps you judge what your final piece will look like (or should look like). Different types of proofs are used for different stages of work.

It is important to build in the time and budget to properly preflight and proof your project at various stages.

Spelling, prices, and proofreading

I can't spell. Honestly! I have a total brain block with words like "accomodate," "embarrased," and "knowlege." I can't remember how they are supposed to look. (Yes, I know they are misspelled here. I did it to prove my point. Did you catch those errors?) That's why it is really important that you do as much as you can to find errors before the job is finished.

Spell check

If the application you are using has a spell check feature, use it. A spell check will look through your document and find those words it doesn't recognize. But that doesn't mean that a spell check will find all spelling mistakes. Consider the following:

Their is knot any thing wrung with this cent tents.

It is utter nonsense. But no spell checker would ever catch it as being misspelled because those are actual words. A spell checker can only find words that it doesn't recognize. But real words in the wrong position won't show up.

This is why it is vital that you add time to send your job to a proof-reader to make sure you haven't used the wrung words.

Prices

A misspelled word is embarrassing. The wrong price could cost you or your client lots of money in angry customers. If you have any pricing information in your project, you must have at least two different people check those prices *before* the job goes out to be printed.

Proofreading

There are ways to automate the proofing process. For instance, I have some automation controls in my page layout program that will look through my documents to make sure I haven't put two spaces between a word.

But you can't totally rely on automation. You must build time into a project to have it properly proofread. Find a proofreader. These are very smart people who know where the commas are supposed to be. They also have incredibly sharp eyes and can see where a wide em space has been inserted instead of the shorter en space.

Preflight

OK, so once you know the words and text are correct, you still have production errors to look for. Perhaps you're working on a spot color job. You wouldn't want any process colors to sneak in. Or you want to make sure that all your images are at the right resolution and color mode.

With a single-page ad, it's pretty simple to check all the elements on the page. But consider a long document with hundreds of elements and images. You really don't want to check all those items individually.

Built-in preflight controls

I once explained to a student that it would be impossible for anyone to read 4-point white text set on a the black area of a color photo. She replied, "Then why did the software let me do it?"

Most page layout software has some sort of preflight controls that check various elements in the document. But not all preflight controls will check for things like text that is too small to be read. The software can't stop you from doing something it doesn't know how to identify.

In the past, Preflight has usually been applied just before a file goes out the door to the print provider. You would run the preflight command and then get a list of any missing fonts, wrong color images, or other problems.

However, one nice feature in InDesign is its Live Preflight feature. Instead of waiting till you're finished working, the Live Preflight continually checks your document for any errors and displays a green mark if everything is OK, and a red mark if it finds problems.

QuarkXPress uses a slightly different approach. It allows you to set a preference to evaluate a file when you open it, save it, output (print) it, or close it.

Professional preflight software

You may use software that doesn't have any preflight controls. For instance, Adobe Illustrator has no built-in preflight at all. If that is the case, you should consider investing in a separate preflight program such as Markzware's FlightCheck Designer (markzware. com). This application looks at all sorts of documents including pdf files.

Monitor proofing

Your monitor is actually your first proofing device. The image on the monitor is sometimes called a **soft proof** because it is the software that controls the appearance of the file.

You can easily judge if all your elements are in position, but you should not rely on your monitor as your only proofing device. You can't judge colors correctly; you can't tell if the colors will output onto the appropriate separate plates; and you can't tell if fonts and vector images will output correctly.

Proofing text

Ordinarily you can just use a desktop printing machine to output text for proofreading. You can also create simple pdf files and have your clients review the text on screen.

But it might be important to know if the point size of text is too small to be read easily. A desktop printing machine won't help you there. Its output resolution is too low to accurately judge fine details in text. If it's important to know exactly what text and vector illustrations will look like, you may want to send the files to a print provider for high-resolution RC paper proofs. You wouldn't want to send an entire book out, but you can send a few sample pages out for tests. This will give you the best idea of whether or not your lines are thick enough to be printed with ink on a press.

Proofing separations

Before you send your file out, it is important to know how the colors are going to separate and if you have too many spot colors. In the old days, I used to print out paper separations from my laser printer and check the colors on the pages.

Today it is much easier to use the built-in separations preview in programs such as Acrobat Professional, Adobe Illustrator, and Adobe InDesign. With just a click, I can turn on and off the process and spot colors in a document. This is a great way to see if you've defined your colors correctly.

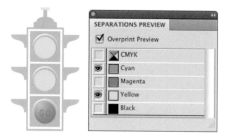

An example of how you can preview the process color separations on screen. Here, the cyan and yellow plates are displayed together while the magenta and black plates are hidden.

Digital color proofs

Digital color proofs are output by color printers such as inkjet, dye-sub, thermal wax, and laser. As mentioned in Chapter 2, the color quality of these proofs varies depending on the type of printer. If you have a very tight color management system in place, you can use these as a preliminary color proof to show the client. But it is never going to be press quality.

Digital proofs are quick and economical. It's easy to go back to the electronic file to make corrections. However, because they are not made from film separations (like laminate proofs; *covered later in this chapter*), they cannot flag certain problems such as moiré patterns or incorrect overprints. They also can't give you information on spot colors. Nonetheless, they are excellent if you only have a monitor and a black-and-white desktop printer to judge your work.

Some print shops use digital color proofs as **contract proofs**, which is a proof of the job used by the print shop to show what the final product must look like. If your job is an expensive four-color process piece or if you need to see precise color, you don't want to use (nor will the print shop agree to use) this kind of proof for matching the color of the finished job.

Overlay proofs

A print shop or service bureau makes **overlay proofs** (sometimes called **color keys**) by taking the color separations and exposing different pieces of film for each color of the project. The pieces of film are colored with the CMYK colors, limited spot colors, or a combination of both. These pieces of film are then placed over each other to form a composite of the final image.

Unfortunately, the film used in overlay proofs has a slight yellow color, so when the layers of film are stacked on top of each other they tend to change the color of the image. Overlay proofs should not be used for proofing when color correction is important. However, they are excellent for flagging moiré patterns (*see Chapter 9*) and other problems with separations.

If you've never seen an overlay proof, ask your print shop if they have an old one you can look at. It's the best lesson on the CMYK process you'll ever have. You can lift up each layer of film to see those dots of cyan, magenta, yellow, and black that I'm always talking about in this book, and see how the combination of the dots creates all the various colors.

Blueline proofs

A print shop makes **blueline proofs** by taking film separations and combining them together into one photographic print. This creates a single page that shows all of the elements in position.

Blueline proofs are quicker and easier to make than overlay proofs and usually cost less. Use a blueline to make sure all the elements are in position, but not to check problems with dot screens or moiré patterns. The benefit of blueline proofs as opposed to a laser print is that the blueline proof is created using the same print processor as the final output. That way if there is a problem with an image or color not printing correctly, you'll see it. A laser proof might not display the problem.

For a project like this book, the print provider makes bluelines of all the signatures for the book (*see Chapter 2*). They fold, sew-bind, and trim them, and send my publisher a complete copy of the book to proof. It looks like the real book, except it's blue (yes, blue-ish paper and blue ink, like a contractor's blueprint) and each signature is separately bound. The production manager and my editor can proof for positioning, typos, page count, and other various features.

Laminate proofs

A print shop or service bureau makes **laminate proofs** from the film separations by taking layers of CMYK toners or spot color material and applying them onto a special base. The layers of color are then laminated together. In the days before digital production, this was the first chance a customer had to see what the job looked like with all the elements in position and in color.

A laminate proof is the closest thing to the finished job, and it represents the most faithful color because the color is produced from the same separations that will make the final printing plates. Unlike overlay proofs, there are no film layers that affect the color of the pages.

Laminate proofs are expensive and take time. Your print shop will tell you if that time and money is worth it. Typically they are used only to proof expensive, full-color jobs. For instance, my publisher might ask for a laminate proof of the cover of this book, but would never ask for a laminate proof of the interior pages.

Some print shops use laminate proofs as **contract proofs** to show what the final print run must look like; if the job doesn't turn out like the contract proof, the customer can ask for the job to be reprinted (but if the project is that important, the client should be at the press check; *see next section*). If the project is to be reproduced in full color, many print shops require a laminate proof of every page, even for an entire book, before they will print the job.

Different print shops use different systems to create their laminate proofs, such as Chromalin, Matchprint, or Agfaproof. The Matchprint brand is so popular that many people refer to a laminate proof as a **matchprint**, regardless of what brand the print shop uses.

Press proofs and press checks

Press proofs are printed samples that are created using the actual plates for the job running on the printing press. The actual paper and ink for the final job are also used. Press proofs are very expensive because they have to set up the entire press as if they were going to print the entire project. You do not need a press proof unless you use a print shop located in another country, in which case you would want to see exactly what the job is going to look like before the entire run is printed.

Big ad agencies, design studios, and publishing houses often send a production person and sometimes the designer to the print shop for a **press check** to make sure the printed pieces are exactly what they want. Typically you would only spend the time on a press check in a four-color job, and in that case the job is usually printed on a four-color press, with four giant rollers, so what comes off at the end is a finished four-color piece. It's amazing.

In a press check, the job is set up on the press and ready to roll. It does roll. As the signatures come off the press, the production person and/or designer look over the pages under a color-corrected light. If the color is not quite right, the press operator can actually push some buttons on a control panel and adjust the ink flow to suit the designer and to match the laminate proof. Maybe it needs more red in the sunset, or less blue in the face—the press operator adjusts it. When everyone is happy with the color, the registration, and all the details, the designer signs a perfect page indicating approval, and the rest of the print run is monitored to match the approved page.

Proofing direct-to-plate

In the **direct-to-plate** process mentioned in Chapter 3, the print provider skips the process of creating film separations. This means they can't make bluelines, color overlays, or laminate proofs, but they can make electronic prepress digital proofs that are different from conventional bluelines, but perform the same function.

If you need to see color, make a digital color proof before going direct-to-plate, or have the print shop make an electronic prepress digital color proof. You can't expect the color in the digital proofs to be as close to the final product as in laminate proofs, but at least you will have a good idea of what to expect.

Fixing film and plates

Once you've created film or plates, what happens if you discover an error? What if you find an incorrect phone number, a misspelled client's name, or maybe you've changed the price? Is there anything you can do? Yes, print providers have always been able to make minor changes to film or plates.

If you discover a mistake after the film or plates have been made, talk to the print shop. Depending on what the mistake is and where it is located on the page, the print shop may still be able to make a correction. If they can't make it, you might have to go back to your electronic file, make the correction, and provide the print shop with new output. Do expect to pay for the service.

And after it's printed?

What if you've printed the entire job and then discover a mistake? It's completely impossible to change it then, right? Well actually not. It just depends on how important the mistake is. If you had 5,000 copies of a book completely printed, bound, and trimmed, and then discover you forgot to put a line of copy on the cover, you can go back to the print shop and have stickers printed up. Then someone manually puts the stickers on all of the covers. It's expensive, but it's possible and it's less expensive than reprinting the entire book. Now, how do you think I know this? Do you think it might have happened to one of my book?

You've surely read publications before that included a small "errata" slip explaining the errors that were discovered after printing. If you have great marketing skills, you can convince the world that the version of your job that includes the mistakes is a collector's item woth thousands of dollars.

And I am positive that somewhere in this book there is a typo that you will catch. However, you never know, with me, what is the the typo and what is the intentional error.

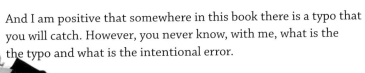

Preflight Checklist

Congratulations, you've made it

through the whole book and are ready to send your job off to be professionally output! Of course you don't want to get a phone call late at night from the print service provider telling you one of your pictures is missing. Or your fonts are styled incorrectly. Or the colors are too dense. And are you sure those colors were set as process, not spot? And the resolution is correct? And what about text that might have reflowed? And are the printer fonts included? And…? *Hold it!* There are too many things to remember all at once!

You're not expected to keep all this in your head. This chapter contains a checklist to help you go through your job in an orderly fashion and make sure everything is correct before you send it to be printed or published.

Your preflight checklist

Use the checklist on the following pages as a guide to make sure your job prints correctly. Blank lines have been added for you to add your own requirements. Feel free to photocopy this checklist and use it for each job. Or download an interactive PDF of the list at: http://www.peachpit.com/designintoprint.

Items marked OPT are optional items that you should consider checking. These are items that will not necessarily cause the job to print incorrectly, but they may confuse the person at the service bureau who opens the file. Rather than get a phone call asking questions, it's better to make sure you don't have any of these items in your file or on your disk.

Materials to be sent

_____	Native files, images, and fonts on disk
_____	Placed images are in the same folder as the files that use those images
_____	Remove all unnecessary files (such as old files, images, fonts, and so on) from the disk OPT
_____	Report from the Collect for Output or Packaging commands
_____	Output specifications form
_____	Hard copy prints of final file
_____	Marked-up proofs for color jobs
_____	Phone number of contact person on label of the disk

_____

_____

_____

_____

_____

Page layout file

_____ Page size is correct

_____ No blank pages in the document except those that have been intentionally left blank   OPT

_____ Page numbers are correct

_____ Unused colors are deleted   OPT

_____ Unused styles are deleted   OPT

_____ Remove elements on the pasteboard   OPT

_____ No overflow text blocks   OPT

_____ Page setup is correct

_____ No elements have been told not to print   OPT

_____ Bleed is applied if necessary

_____

_____

_____

_____

Colors

_____ Number of colors has been verified with paper separations or separations preview

_____ No colors are defined using more than 300 percent total ink (check with the print provider or publication for the amount they prefer)

_____ Spot color names are correct

_____ Knockout elements are correct

_____ No actual artwork in the job uses the color "registration"

_____ All spot colors have been converted to process for a four-color process job

_____

_____

_____

_____

Placed or inserted images

_____ No pictures are listed as missing

_____ All RGB images have been converted to CMYK
Or
Print provider will convert RGB images to CMYK (check with them!)

_____ Grayscale and color images are at their correct resolution (2 x linescreen = _____)
300 ppi is the most common resolution

_____ Images have not been enlarged so the effective resolution is too low

_____ Line art has been scanned as 1-bit, not grayscale

_____ Line art is at proper resolution (up to 1200 ppi)

_____ Vector illustrations have not been reduced until their elements are too small

_____ No pictures are on unused master pages   OPT

_____

_____

_____

_____

Text and outlines

_____ Small typefaces do not have color tints (check with the print shop for the correct specifications for colored type)

_____ Small line weights do not have color tints (check with the print shop for the correct specifications for colored lines)

_____ No fonts are listed as missing

_____ If fonts are not embedded in the PDF, a note has been added stating what font is necessary for printing

_____

_____

_____

_____

_____

Glossary

Moving your designs into print can be a bit frightening. And you may feel out of your element when print providers and production managers start using all their jargon.

The following is a glossary that I obtained from Markzware's user manual for their FlightCheck Professional. It covers much of the material in this book as well as some more advanced topics that you may encounter. Markzware has been kind enough to allow me to reprint it here for you.

absolute path

The location of a particular computer file as described subdirectory by subdirectory. *See also relative path.*

actual resolution

The resolution of an image as it was saved from a scan or digital camera or image editing program before any reductions or enlargements have been applied in the page layout program. *See effective resolution.*

additive color

The color model of computer monitors, movie projectors, and the human eye, in which the primary colors (red, green, and blue), when added together, produce white. Sometimes called transmissive color. *See also RGB; subtractive color.*

alpha channel

An extra channel of data. Image editing applications will use alpha channels typically to store information (both eight-bit grayscale and vector) on masks, clipping paths, and spot colors.

ASCII data

The initials stand for American Standard Code for Information Interchange. A standard method of representing text as numerical data designed originally to be used by Teletype and Linotype machines. The original set consists of 128 characters; this was expanded in the 1980s to 256 characters. Those two sets are also called seven-bit data and eight-bit data respectively. Even today, "ASCII data" is used most often to refer to the original seven-bit character set.

background color

The background color of an object in desktop publishing applications is the color that object is filled with. All objects with the exception of lines have a background color. Historically, elements with a background color of "None" have caused problematic output, particularly when they are the bottom-most element on the page.

banding

An artifact caused by digital output that makes a gradient appear to have discrete tonal steps or bands instead of a smooth graduation in tonality. The artifact was more pronounced in PostScript Level 1 than in subsequent implementations, but it can still be found in some large-format output.

Bézier curves

The method used by PostScript to define the curvature of vector paths. (The name comes from Pierre Bézier, the French mechanical engineer who developed the approach for computer-aided drafting applications in the 1970s.) In desktop publishing usage, these curves can be recognized by the presence of control points with manipulable handles.

binary data

Data that use all eight bits of a byte, as opposed to those that use only seven of those bits. The distinction was important more so in the past than in the present; many of the earlier computer networks used the eighth bit for error control and so could only handle seven-bit (or "ASCII") data.

bitmap

(1) The electronic representation of a page described by a series of bits (binary digits with a value of either zero or one) that are meant to be output as dots that are either black or white.

(2) The electronic representation of an image described by a series of bits or pixels.

bitmapped font

See screen font.

bitmapped image

(1) A monochrome raster image; line art.

(2) A raster image, whether monochrome, grayscale, or color.

bleed

Additional image (typically an extra pica or a quarter-inch) appearing outside the nominal printing area to allow for the mechanical tolerances of the trimming process.

clipping path

A mask applied to, and usually saved with, a specific graphic which hides unwanted parts of the image. A clipping path can be as simple as a square frame for the picture or as complicated as an intricate knockout and can be described by either vector or raster data.

CMYK

The initials for cyan, magenta, yellow, and black, which are the inks used in process-color printing. According to color theory, the first three inks added together make black; however, black ink is also needed to make up for such physical shortcomings as total ink density.

color separation

The result of filtering a full-color image into its primary components in order to print in full color using only the four process inks. *See process color.*

complex path

When there are an excessive number of control points along a path in a vector image, older PostScript interpreters might bog down or fail to render the image. The path would then be simplified by removing unnecessary control points.

compression

Decreasing the size of a file for storage or transfer. Software such as WinZip and StuffIt are commonly used to compress files with no loss of image quality.

continuous tone

A raster image that includes tonalities; a grayscale image.

CPU

The initials stand for central processing unit. The part of the computer that directs most of the system's activity including any arithmetic calculations and comparisons. The CPU extracts instructions from memory and executes them.

crop marks

Traditionally, the term refers to the marks used to show what part of an image is to be cropped and printed. The term is also used to describe the trim marks of a printed piece.

cropping

The act of defining the precise area of an image that is to appear on the printed page, not unlike using scissors to trim out the desired area of a photograph.

default

This term is used to describe settings or functions which computer hardware or software will automatically use unless the operator specifies otherwise.

DPI

The initials stand for "dots per inch." A measure of digital resolution, whether applied to a raster image, a computer monitor, or a printed page. Devices can have different horizontal and vertical resolutions.

duotone

A two-color halftone produced from a one-color photograph (or other continuous-tone image) by applying its grayscale values in two different ink colors.

effective resolution

The resolution at which a raster image will be printed. This is the result of the image's actual resolution divided by the enlargement or reduction factor at which it is to be output. For example, a 72 DPI image output at 25% would have an effective resolution of 288 DPI. *See also actual resolution.*

embedded file

A file whose data have been included completely within another file, as opposed to a linked file.

embedded font

A font stored within the document (typically a PDF) that uses it and not available for the operating system to use elsewhere.

EPS

The initials stand for "encapsulated PostScript," a file format that can contain both text and image data and that can be shared across most computer platforms and most desktop publishing applications.

facing pages

When a left-hand page and a right-hand page face each other in a layout, they are said to be facing pages. Also called "reader's spreads." Other common ways to display a multipage document are in continuous single pages and in imposition order.

flat

A sheet of dimensionally stable plastic, usually goldenrod in color, used in traditional lithography. Film negatives are combined (stripped) onto flats before plates are made. The flat is then used to expose (burn) the film images onto the printing plates.

folding dummy

A dummy is a "mock-up" made with the correct size, format, and paper of the final printed document. A folding dummy is used to show the page layout for the film stripping department.

font

The complete set of characters in a typeface. Every font has a unique weight, style, and sometimes size.

FPO

The initials stand for "for position only." An element used as a placeholder, usually a low-resolution raster image that needs to be replaced by its high-resolution counterpart when the document is output.

GIF

The initials stand for "graphic interchange format." A group of file formats designed primarily for exchanging raster images across computer platforms, more appropriate for images meant to be viewed on monitors than for commercial printing.

gradient

A gradual change from one tonality to another, as when black fades to white. Also called gradation, dégradé, blend, and vignette.

grayscale

An adjective meant to describe raster images made up of varying tonalities, or levels of gray, as opposed to line art. When a grayscale image is output, its levels of gray are normally converted to black-and-white halftone dots varying in size to approximate each different level.

H&J

The initials stand for "hyphenation and justification," the traditional typographical process of determining how to end a line of type whereby the last word on the line, if it doesn't fit, is broken (hyphenated) and the leftover horizontal space is distributed across the words in that line in order for the line to set to full measure (justified). On the computer, this process is controlled by sophisticated algorithms supported by an exceptions dictionary.

hairline rule

In traditional printing, a line (or rule) a quarter of a point thick. PostScript defines the hairline, however, as a stroke of one device pixel in weight; when the device outputs 2540 pixels per inch, as in the case of commercial printing, such a stroke is almost invisible.

halftone

An image reproduced on the printing press by breaking down its original continuous tone or grayscale into a pattern of dots of varying size. Light areas of the original image are printed with small dots, darker areas or shadows with large dots.

highlights

The lightest areas in a photograph or illustration. The other areas are referred to as midtones and shadows.

ICC profile

The initials stand for International Color Consortium, an industry-wide committee that establishes standards for color management. These profiles are mathematical descriptions of how specific devices behave when outputting color; their purpose is to promote standardized color-matching among all combinations of input, display, and output equipment.

imagesetter

A device that takes interpreted PostScript code that has been rendered into a rasterized format and outputs that to create images on film or paper.

InDesign

A page layout software application used for creating print-ready publications from Adobe Systems Inc.

indexed color

A color system that uses information from a file or from software as a pointer to a "look-up table" of colors rather than specifying a color directly. Color specified from a 24-bit palette but displayed in an 8-bit system is indexed color. Indexed color is not suitable for commercial printing.

ink density

The total amount of ink present on a printed sheet, usually measured at darkest shadow of an image. Depending on the type of paper, the type of press, and the formulation of the inks, the maximum ink density that a sheet can hold varies generally between 260% and 340%. This means that an element printing at full strength in all four process colors (a total ink density of 400%) would exceed the physical limits of all known offset lithography and would really annoy the people running the press.

interpolation

An algorithm applied by applications that edit raster images when increasing the size of such an image. These algorithms attempt to add new pixels that are similar but not identical to the original pixels, so the color and tonality of the new pixels are interpolated from those of the original pixels nearby.

JDF

The initials stand for Job Definition Format, an electronic job ticket meant to be used in conjunction with PDFs and other files in an automated digital workflow to assure predictable and consistent output results.

JPEG

The initials stand for Joint Photographic Experts Group, the industry-wide committee that developed this file format, which is referred to technically as JFIF. It is a method of compressing raster data into files considerably smaller than the original, but at the expense of losing pixels that are determined to be cognitively unimportant. Repeated application of the JPEG algorithm to a file will result in visual artifacts and degradation of the image.

kerning

The adjustment of spacing between certain letter pairs, A and V for example, to obtain a more pleasing appearance.

keyline

An outline drawn or set on artwork showing the size and position of an illustration or halftone.

L*a*b color

A color model and proposed international standard that defines each color as a product of its luminance (L), its position on the green-red axis (a), and its position on the blue-yellow axis (b). L*a*b color has a wider gamut than have the RGB and CMYK models and can be applied without reference to an output profile. Sometimes called CIE L*a*b in honor of the Commission Internationale d'Éclairage.

landscape

The orientation of an image or page where its width is greater than its height, so called because images of landscapes have to be turned sideways in order to fit onto the page of a normal book. *See also portrait.*

layers

Tiers or levels of a document that allow you to work on some elements without affecting other elements of the same document. You can hide the layers of a document or make them visible.

leading

The vertical space between one line of type and the next. Computer graphics will express this spacing in terms of points, the traditional measure, or as a percentage of the size of the type being used.

ligature

Letters that are joined together as a single unit of type, such as "fl" and "fi."

line art

An image with no tonalities, such that it can be represented by a bitmap or monochrome file. The opposite of continuous tone.

linked file

A file whose data are meant to be included in the output of another file where the two exist as separate files. The main file contains either a relative or absolute pointer to the ancillary file whose path must be valid at the time of output if the linked file is to print correctly.

LPI

The initials stand for "lines per inch," also called "ruling"; it is the measure of halftone screens. The finer the ruling (the higher the LPI), the more details can be preserved from the original image.

margin guides

Most desktop publishing applications allow the user to specify the "live area" of a page by defining the amounts of margin to be allowed on all four sides.

mask

A mask allows you to isolate and protect areas of an image as you apply color changes, filters, or other effects to the rest of the image. When you select part of an image, the area that is not selected is masked, or protected from editing. You can also use masks for complex image editing such as gradually applying color or filter effects to an image.

master page

A template that can be used to create uniform pages throughout your document. Anything placed on a master page will appear on each page derived from that master page throughout the document.

midtones

The area of an image in the middle of the tonal range, neither highlights nor shadows.

moiré pattern

The result, often visually objectionable, of superimposing one screen on top of another. Moirés occur in multicolor halftones and when a halftone is rescreened (taken from a previously printed copy instead of a continuous-tone original).

monochrome image

Another term for line art. The image consists of a single color with no tints or gradations.

nested image

An image file placed within another image file. If the nested image is embedded, there should be no difficulty outputting the entire image; if it is only linked, it might be missing when the file it is nested in is output.

one-bit image

See bitmapped image.

OpenType font

A cross-platform typographical specification incorporating Unicode and other innovations. It is too new to be used on some flavors of Windows or most versions of the classic (pre–OS X) Macintosh operating system.

OPI

The initials stand for "open prepress interface." An extension to PostScript that allows designers to use low-resolution FPO images during the production of desktop-publishing files, which are replaced automatically by high-resolution versions of the same images when the work is output for commercial printing. Sometimes called PostScript-5. Other methods that achieve the same end are DCS and APR.

orientation

See landscape and portrait.

overprinting

A printing technique, also called surprinting, in which a graphic element is printed on top of another element without knocking out the lower element. Transparent and semi-transparent inks are used in this technique because they blend to form new colors with the inks below them.

page geometry

In desktop publishing, a skeletal representation of a page with the various graphic elements therein shown as keylined shapes.

paper gap

An option in many printer drivers to allow for extra space between one page and another when the pages are being output to rolls of paper or film.

paper offset

An option in many printer drivers to allow for extra blank space on the left side of the output material.

pasteboard

In desktop publishing applications, the area outside of a working page where you can store objects that are not yet positioned on the page.

PDF

As used by Adobe Acrobat, the acronym stands for Portable Document Format.

PICT

A format commonly used on the Macintosh to store color or grayscale previews of EPS files. The format is more appropriate for system-level uses than for commercial printing.

pixel

The term is a contraction of "picture element," the smallest unit of a raster image. A monochrome pixel, being either black or white, is described by a single bit; a pixel in 256 levels of grayscale is described by an entire byte. Sandee's cat is named Pixel.

pixel depth

The amount of information contained in one pixel. One-bit is simple black and white; eight-bit contains 256 grayscale levels, 24-bit contains three channels (either RGB or L*a*b) of 256 levels each, and so on.

plug-in

An auxiliary utility that extends the functionality of larger applications. All Adobe applications use the term plug-ins to describe these utilities. Markzware's Q2ID is such a plug-in for InDesign.

PNG

The initials stand for "portable network graphics." A format for raster images meant to supplant GIF.

portrait

The orientation of an image or page where its height is greater than the width. *See also landscape.*

postflighting

The process of analyzing interpreted or processed files (such as PostScript, PDF, DCS2, TIFF/IT, and fully rasterized data) for quality control in a digital prepress workflow.

PostScript

A page description language. PostScript was introduced by Adobe Systems Inc. in 1985 to provide a high-level, device-independent page description language to control a wide range of different output devices. Since then PostScript has become the standard language that drives desktop printers and imagesetters.

PostScript Type 1 font

A font consisting of two files: one, the printer font, which contains a description of the characters in terms of vectors, and the other, the screen font, which contains bitmaps of all the characters at one or more specific point-sizes.

PPD

The initials stand for PostScript Printer Description; a file that contains information on the specific capabilities of an individual PostScript printer.

PPI

The initials stand for "pixels per inch," a measure of resolution for raster images.

preflighting

The examination, verification, and attestation of desktop publishing documents prior to sending them to be output by a RIP.

printer font

A typeface described in terms of vector data, which is what Post-Script printers use to print type.

process color

A method of printing in full color by means of four superimposed inks: cyan, magenta, yellow, and black.

quadtone

A method of printing in which a grayscale image is printed using four colors to give greater tonal range or to achieve a colorized effect.

QuarkXPress

A page layout application from Quark Inc. used for creating publications.

raster image

(1) The file of single-bit pixels produced by a RIP.

(2) Any image comprised of pixels, not vectors.

raster image processor (RIP)

The device that produces a digital image of a printing plate by calculating from a series of instructions the bitmap of all text and graphics. PostScript instructions are currently the industry standard. Three major versions of PostScript have been released (Level

1, Level 2, and PostScript 3) that have generally been built into the RIP hardware, thus fixing a particular RIP at a particular level of PostScript.

rasterization

(1) The process of converting page description language into the particular pattern of dots (the raster image) that will make up the image of a page on the printing plate.

(2) The process of converting vector images or fonts into a pixel-based illustration.

reader's spreads

The layout of pages that mimics the way a reader would view the pages bound in a book.

registration

The correct positioning of an image, especially when printing one color on or near another.

registration color

A color made up of all the colors used in a multicolor printing job.

registration marks

Targets used in multicolor printing to position the paper for correct registration. The marks are usually crosses or circles printed in registration color outside of the live area.

relative path

A way of specifying a file's location within the disk structure by describing the path to it from the local directory downward. On Macintosh platforms, the symbol ":" stands for the local directory and "::" stands for the parent of the local directory; on Windows platforms, that shorthand is represented by ".\" and "..\" respectively. *See also absolute path.*

resolution

The measure of how detailed an image is. It is expressed a number of ways: for a raster file by the raw number of pixels it contains, for a computer screen by the number of pixels in a linear inch

(PPI), for a laser printer by the number of dots printed in a linear inch (DPI), for a scanner by the number of pixels per inch (PPI) or the number of pixels per square millimeter (RES), and for a halftone by the number of lines of halftone dots per inch (LPI).

RGB

This acronym stands for the primary additive colors red, green, and blue. RGB is the standard color model used for monitors and televisions. This color model should be avoided when creating documents for print, which uses the CMYK model.

RIP

See raster image processor.

runaround

Type set such that it fits around a picture or other graphic element of the page design. Also called text wrap.

screen angles

The direction of the lines or rows of dots in a halftone screen. In multicolor printing, the superimposition of one color's halftone screen onto another color's will create a moiré pattern; by using optimal screen angles, the amount of moiré can be minimized.

screen font

A typeface represented as a bitmap at one or more specific pointsizes; this is used for displaying the font on computer monitors.

separation

See also color separation.

shadows

The darkest parts of an image. *See also highlights, midtones.*

spot color

A ink other than, and often in addition to, the four process inks; also, a color that is printed in an ink of that specific color rather than built from a combination of process-color tints. Every spot color requires its own printing plate.

spreads

See reader's spreads.

stylesheet

A collection of formatting attributes meant to be applied to a paragraph, a group of characters, or page elements.

substrate

The material onto which ink, toner, or pigment is applied. The most common substrate is paper; other materials include label stock, plastics, synthetic papers, and overhead transparencies.

subtractive color

The color model of ink on paper, in which the primary colors (cyan, magenta, and yellow), when taken away, make white. Sometimes called reflective color. *See also CMYK; additive color.*

suitcase

A special kind of Macintosh file in which a screen font, or a group of screen fonts, can be stored and be made available to the operating system.

text linking

The method of creating a single text stream to flow through designated pages or text boxes. Text boxes can be linked in any sequential order, allowing text to flow from one text box to another. Sometimes called threading.

thumbnails

Small versions of an image or page layout. The small versions of complete pages may be viewed in most page layout applications and can also be printed directly from those applications.

TIFF

The initials stand for "tagged image file format." A common, cross-platform file format for raster image data used for monochrome, grayscale, and color images.

TIFF/IT

The initials stand for "tagged image file format for image technology." An international standard, ISO 12639, based on the TIFF specification and broadened in order to transmit complete pages of raster data.

tiling

Printing a file by sections across several pieces of paper that must then be assembled like tiles, the way billboards are made.

tint

The effect of adding white to a hue or of applying a halftone screen to an area of solid color.

trapping

The term refers colloquially to enlarging ("spreading") or reducing ("choking") an area of color so that it overlaps slightly with a neighboring color. This is done so that no gaps appear on printed sheets that are slightly out of register.

trim marks

Hairline strokes placed outside of the live area to show where the finished printed piece should be trimmed out of the press sheet.

trim size

The size of a printed document after it has been cut out of the press sheet but before it is folded or subjected to other bindery operations. The trim size should in most cases equal the page size of a document.

tritone

A method of printing in which a grayscale image is printed using three colors to give greater tonal range or to achieve a colorized effect.

TrueType font

A font format that combines into a single file the information used to display type on a monitor with the information used to print to an output device.

Type 1 font

See PostScript Type 1 font.

vector image

An image described in mathematical terms of points and curves. Vector images can represent both grayscale and line art but, because they have no inherent resolution, they may be enlarged without any degradation of the image. *See also Bézier curves.*

vignette

(1) An image not enclosed in a definite border.

(2) A gradient.

workflow

A broad term referring to the hardware, software, sequence of steps employed in the production of digital printing, and the effects of their interactions.

WYSIWYG

The initials stand for "what you see is what you get."

XTension

A utility, tool, or plug-in that offers additional capabilities to QuarkXPress. Markzware's ID2Q is such an XTension.

▶ INDEX

L

WATCH
READ
CREATE

Meet Creative Edge.

A new resource of unlimited books, videos and tutorials for creatives from the world's leading experts.

Creative Edge is your one stop for inspiration, answers to technical questions and ways to stay at the top of your game so you can focus on what you do best—being creative.

All for only $24.99 per month for access—any day any time you need it.

peachpit.com/creativeedge